CONCILIUM
Religion in the Seventies

CONCILIUM

Religion in the Seventies

Volume 63: Pastoral Theology

DEMOCRATIZATION OF THE CHURCH

Edited by
Alois Muller

Herder and Herder

1971
HERDER AND HERDER NEW YORK
232 Madison Avenue, New York 10016

CONTENTS

PART II
DOCUMENTATION CONCILIUM

Editorial

THE concept "democratization of the Church" certainly gives rise to many questions and even misunderstandings, but this should surely act as an incentive to us to think very carefully about the underlying reality and to express it in such a way that it cannot easily be misunderstood. If we take the literal translation of the word as "power" or "rule" of the "people" as our basis for discussion, then we are bound to agree that democracy cannot be applied either to life in contemporary society or to the Church. Both in human society and in the community of the Church, there can be no question of anyone "ruling" or having "power" over anyone else, unless this is understood as the exalted Kyrios or Lord ruling in power over the Church. But even this rule of Christ over the Church is the exact opposite of what we usually mean by rule or power: "The Son of Man came not to be served but to serve, and to give his life as a ransom for many" (Mark 10. 45).

If, however, despite the obvious possibility of misunderstanding, the term democratization is used in the pastoral number of *Concilium* in connection with the Church, this is relatively easy to explain. In our opinion, there is as yet no other word which expresses in a better way what is meant by this concept, namely, an interrelationship of principles, attitudes, patterns of behaviour and legal forms current in society which are intended to overcome man's alienation.

In the present number of *Concilium*, then, an attempt is made to throw some light on this problem of the democratization of

7

the Church. The first step is made by a specialist in political science, who shows how the idea of democracy first arose, how this idea, together with the political reality of democracy, developed in the course of history, how democracy has been expressed in various ways in modern times and how it is being questioned and differently understood nowadays in the East and in the West. We have given such great freedom and scope to this author because we are convinced that a knowledge of these "profane" sciences can only be of benefit to theologians.

The second step is made by a New Testament exegete, who attempts to show that there are lines which run from the New Testament to the democratization of the Church. In a third article, a systematic theologian sets out in what sense and under what conditions a democratization of the Church might be possible. Our original intention was that this article should be followed by a contribution on the need for permanent synodal structures at all levels within the Church and on the ways in which this might be accomplished. This was unfortunately made impossible by the illness of a colleague and the result is an inevitable gap in the structure of this number of the journal. This omission can to some extent be remedied by examining the contents of *Concilium* of October 1970 (American edition, vol. 58), in which the structures of the Church in the world of today, with special reference to the lowest level of life in the Church, that of the local Christian community, are discussed in some detail. We should therefore like to draw attention to that issue.

Certain factors which form a constitutive element in the democratization of any society are then investigated to see if they can be applied to the Church—publicity and communication in the Church, the choice and appointment of those holding office, the distribution of authority, training in democracy and democratic forms of life in the Church. The Dutch Pastoral Council is then considered as a democratic assembly in the Church.

The content and meaning of office in a democratic Church is not dealt with in a special contribution. This is because the life and ministry of the priest in the world of today were discussed in detail in the March 1969 number of *Concilium* (American edition, vol. 43) and the April 1971 number will be devoted to the office of Peter in the Church.

What should therefore be clear from all these different contributions is that the Church cannot simply remedy the deficiencies in her own structures or adapt herself by an uncritical acceptance or imitation of a liberal or socialist form of democratic government and administration of the kind practised in the so-called secular sphere. What can, however, be recognized is that there is a great affinity between modern democratic ways of thinking and democratic social structures on the one hand and the spirit of the Gospel on the other. It is furthermore obvious that a radical democratization of the Church has become urgently necessary if the Church is to be accepted as credible and is to act efficiently in contemporary society. What is more, precisely because Jesus' words and actions are the constant preoccupation of Christians today in their attitude of conversion and renewal, it is even possible that new models for men's life together in the community may be realized in the Church and that these may, within certain limits, act as examples for so-called secular society.

ALOIS MÜLLER
NORBERT GREINACHER
KARL LEHMANN

PART I
ARTICLES

Heinrich Schneider

Democracy: The Idea
and the Reality

"THE factor which, more than any other, acts like a raw nerve in
the crucial development currently taking place in the Catholic
Church is the fact that life in the Church is not governed by the
principles of democracy as understood in modern times."[1] In
these terms the "Bensberg circle" makes its own ideas which are
in any case circulating in the intellectual climate of the time.
According to Wilhelm Hennis the single word "democratization" provides "the most concise formula in which to sum up the
general tendency of all the demands of the time that the social
structure of the world in which we live shall be altered".[2] All too
frequently concise formulas serve to conceal the full range and
complexity of the problems they stand for. When so many use the
term "democracy" as though it actually expressed the very
essence of all that is good in social life[3] it is time to introduce
distinctions and clarifications.

I. DEMOCRACY IN THE GREEK POLIS

Democracy is a political concept. It derives from the world of
the Greek *polis*. Even modern ideas on democracy refer back

[1] *Demokratisierung der Kirche in der Bundesrepublik Deutschland. Ein
Memorandum deutscher Katholiken*, ed. by the Bensberg Circle (Mainz,
1970), pp. 55, 73.
[2] W. Hennis, *Demokratisierung—Zur Problematik eines Begriffs*
(Cologne, 1970), p. 9.
[3] Cf. E. von Kahler, "Das Problem der Demokratie", *Synopsis. Festgabe
für Alfred Weber* (Heidelberg, 1948), p. 105.

again and again to the *polis*. Already in the period of the *polis* certain basic problems had already come to be recognized and expressed with regard to the real meaning of democracy. The *polis* was based primarily on the institution of certain rules of human conduct which were initially binding upon all the members of a society made up of the nobility and heads of families. Subsequently the peasants, tradespeople and finally all freeborn citizens came to be recognized as active participants in this social organization, though certainly this recognition was not won without a struggle. Thus the *polis* finally came to be the concern of all citizens acting in common. Political forms and ways of life came increasingly to be recognized as the subject of acts of self-determination carried out in concert.

Democrateia means "government of the people". The Athenians sought to establish it on a sound basis primarily by submitting all important decisions to the assembly of the people. They further prescribed that all those commissioned to conduct the various branches of public business should be given only limited mandates to perform specific tasks, that they should hold these only for a limited time, and that they should be subject to constant supervision. Frequently the way in which such commissions were obtained was by lot. It was intended that official authority should never become autonomous or independent of control. From this alone certain problems arise with regard to the basic forms of the society involved.[4]

First, such a system does not admit of any professionalism being evolved in political life. Every individual must be in a position to discharge the tasks of official life as these fall to him. Matters on which decisions have to be taken must be evident to all, and should not require any particular specialized knowledge. Second, such a system necessarily presupposes that the citizens can be counted upon constantly and actively to engage themselves in political life. They must be able to absent themselves from the necessities of earning their living and from their private callings, as well as being prepared and in a position to play an active and

[4] Obviously this represents an idealized simplification for the sake of establishing a type. For instance, a point that is not taken into account is that even in the democratic epoch the supreme offices in Athens were open only to those who belonged to the upper class.

intelligent part in the affairs of the *polis*. This presupposes that they have both independent means and education, and for this reason the classical authors of philosophy were against democracy—even apart from the fact that it was always only a minority of the Attic Greeks who possessed the rights of citizenship. Direct assistance was needed in the form of daily allowances in order to make it possible for them to fulfil their duties as citizens. And the expenses of this were met through wars or contributions on the part of the satellite states to the maritime confederacy. For all the dwellers in Attic Greece it was all the more true that democracy was too expensive in view of the total resources which the society as a whole could provide.

"*Democrateia*" is a composite word. Its constituent elements point to tensions which found expression right from the outset. The essential element in democracy—the equality of the citizens in their right to political self-determination and to a voice in political decisions—only achieved its current significance at a very late stage, and this went hand in hand with a change in the meaning of politics itself.[5] Initially the forms of political life were worked out in a pre-existing framework which remained constantly in force, that namely of nomos. In the conditions *a priori* imposed by this "nomistic" situation the applications which were actually made had the same binding force as the nomos itself. But, in the process of time, the more awareness grew of the possibility of working out forms of political association which were autonomous, the more this pre-existing nomistic framework lost its validity as a motivating force. Now it is only as a result of this that the question of who is to replace this as providing the supreme standard of judgment by assuming the position of decisive authority (*krateia*) comes to be of decisive importance.

In accordance with this, the slogan of "Isonomia", which belongs to the "nomistic" period, and which signifies equality of political rights for all, is aimed at maintaining or restoring a justice that is binding upon all in the life of the community against the arbitrary decisions of the tyrant. The popular assembly was strengthened so that it could effectively control and correct the official leadership of the nobility. The central concern here

[5] Cf. C. Meier, *Entstehung des Begriffs Demokratie* (Frankfurt/M., 1970), pp. 7–69.

was the preservation of the pre-existing nomos. It is only in the later "kratistic" period that the word democracy becomes current coin. *Krateia* now means power to shape and control the political order. Already in the history of Greek democracy, therefore, we can discern that tension between the supreme authority in the order of justice and the supreme authority in the government of the state which is also of concern to later democratic thought.

A similar tension is also to be found in the concept of the demos. This signifies the union of the citizens, but at the same time the common people as opposed to the upper classes. Democratic conceptions assign control of affairs to the majority, and invariably it is the "lower orders" who constitute the great majority, so that, for instance, Aristotle defines democracy in terms of its content as government by those who have no possessions.[6] Now if we accord its true value to the "kratistic" character of *krateia* we shall understand that for Aristotle "democracy" had to signify something like "dictatorship of the proletariat". There is, then, a shift of meaning here. On the one hand democracy is taken to mean the union of all equals as upholders of public affairs, in which sense it claims to be universal and above all factional divisions. On the other hand, however, it is also used as a watchword standing for the emancipation of the under-privileged classes. Now this duality of meaning likewise remains significant for later ages.

Thus the Athenian democracy left a twofold legacy to later ages. First it acted as an archetype for the politics of emancipation, for "left-wing" orientations of thought and action right down to the present day.[7] On the other hand, however, it also served as a starting-point for developing a philosophical concept of the common weal which is likewise presented as the self-determination of free men to fulfil their human potentialities in common.

This is, in fact, the fruit of Aristotle's philosophy of the *polis*. The fully developed form of the *polis*, in which the possibilities

---

[6] Aristotle, *Politics* III, 18 (1279b ff.).

[7] For a contemporary example of "left wing" emancipatory democracy cf., e.g., W. D. Narr, "Modell einer demokratischen Gesellschaft", *Blätter für deutsche und internationale Politik* 14 (1969), pp. 712–26. Cf. further R. Mühnl, "Rechts und links als politische Grundkategorien", *ibid.*, 12 (1967), pp. 1166–76.

of shaping and constituting it in the best possible way are realized, is the *politeia*. In the thought of Aristotle this expression
signifies the institution of the *polis* in general. But it also
signifies that "good" factor which is the opposite of dictatorship
by the proletariat, namely that "order" in which all free men
will to exercise dominion for the sake of freedom and the fulfilling of human life in such a way that this dominion no longer
has the character of a one-sided controlling of affairs in the
interests of a particular person, group or class, and therefore
signifies something different from dominion as universally understood elsewhere. In dominion, in this sense, man precisely as man
is the subject of the form of life to be lived in common. It constitutes the "intelligent society" in which the human being can
realize his own potentialities, seeing that he is, of his very nature,
at once *zôon lógon échon* and *zôon politikon*.[8]

For Aristotle this in no sense excludes the fact that there are
different degrees of competence for leadership and responsibility,
and that these are determined by according the intellectual and
moral qualities of the particular individual concerned. Nevertheless, between the two viewpoints, Aristotle's definition of what
actually is and the "emancipatory" conception of what must be,
there is a certain connection so long as the "emancipatory" ideas
do not remain circumscribed by class interests, and provided that
"the weaker" really do "seek after justice and equality".[9]

II. How Democracy was Understood at the Beginning of the New Age

The time of the *polis* is past. The function of the democratic
conception has changed. For the Greeks the term pointed to a
reality actually experienced. For the moderns democracy in its
primary meaning is rather an ideal. This is the interpretation
upheld by Giovanni Sartoris,[10] and in support of his argument he
can point to the multiplicity of institutional projects which have
been propagated by man as the modern equivalent to the *"polis"*

[8] Cf. Joachim Ritter, *Metaphysik und Politik* (Frankfurt/M., 1969), especially pp. 57 ff., 106 ff.   [9] Aristotle, *op. cit.*, VI, 3 (1318 b 4).
[10] G. Sartori, "Democracy", *International Encyclopedia of the Social
Sciences* IV (1968), p. 116. Cf. G. Sartori, *Democrazia e Definizione*
(Bologna, 1958²).

democracy, ranging from the state based on liberal and democratic representation to the Soviet Republic, from the model of the "People's democracy" to federalist systems based on anarchist or radical ideas. Conversely, the opponents of the present-day forms of government who arise at various times vehemently contest their claim to be democratic. Although the Church has been recommended to come to terms with the "understanding of democracy of the new age" in the singular, it seems that we can speak only in vague generalizations of any such understanding.

In the new age, right up to the era of the French Revolution, the actual term itself was current only in learned circles, and even then, up to four hundred years ago, had a uniformly negative connotation as used among the most influential thinkers of the time.[11] Thus it was used as a battle cry of the left wing, as expressing the essence of all that was opposed to absolutism, authoritarianism in government and (for the worker movement) the class dominion of the *bourgeois*. Any positive ideas derive their orientation straight from the prototype of antiquity or from constitutional models which seem immediately to correspond to this (ranging from the Swiss cantons to the Paris communes). In all this the idea of the sovereignty of the people was upheld in opposition to the power of the princes or the propertied classes.

Precisely the same idea reappears in the eighteenth century in yet another context, that namely of American republicanism. The constitution of the U.S.A. is also based upon the will of the people, although the authors of this were very far from intending any adaptation of the principle of democracy in the sense in which the term was generally employed at the time.[12] Meanwhile the linguistic usage has undergone a change. The republic after the American pattern and the parliamentary constitution of the state count as democratic, as "representative democracy".

The combination of the principle of the sovereignty of the people with universal parliamentary suffrage and the other institutions belonging to the civic constitution in which power is

[11] W. Hennis, *op. cit.*, p. 27, n. 32, referring to R. P. Palmer, "Notes on the Use of the Word 'Democracy' 1789–1799", *Political Science Quarterly* 68 (1933), p. 204; C. B. Macpherson, *The Real World of Democracy* (London, 1966).
[12] E. Fraenkel, *Das amerikanische Regierungssystem* (Cologne and Opladen, 1960), pp. 39 ff.

distributed is not, according to the ideas which have predominated up till now in the Western world, a distortion of democracy, but rather a purification of it, or at least the rational
application of the basic idea of democracy to modern conditions.
For these are such that the only way in which it appears possible
for the people to have a share in the process of decision-making
has been through representative organs. And the only way in
which it has seemed possible to make sure of guarding against
the dangers of the era of the masses has been through constitutional safeguards (basic rights, protection of minorities).

Admittedly critics object that this has had the effect of making
those concerned betray the essence of democracy; that they have
reduced it to its merely formal aspect and in particular surrendered the claim that the people shall be accorded the right to
self-determination in the widest possible sense. In other words
they have compromised with the prolongation of the dichotomy
between rulers and ruled. But this is a biased criticism. We
would misunderstand the nature of constitutional democracy if
we were to interpret it as the result of a defeatist self-surrender
on the part of movements which are democratic in the radical
sense. Constitutional democracy has a basis in the history of
institutions and ideas which is all its own. This lays down the
principle that all political power to govern is official power.[13] It
is bound up with a predetermined complex of tasks which the
possessors of such power are bound to fulfil in an appropriate
manner, and for which they are obliged to answer. In Anglo-
Saxon circles, and above all those influenced by the ideas of John
Locke, "government" is considered to be entrusted merely with
the faithful protecting of human rights, these rights continuing
in substance to be under the control of the citizens as trustees.[14]
But this is due simply to the fact that a more ancient idea has
been translated into the modern one. Government is bound up
with the common weal and justice as well as with the consensus
of the ruled.[15]

[13] W. Hennis, "Amtsgedanke und Demokratiebegriff", *Staatsverfas-
sung und Kirchennordnung, Festschrift für R. Smend* (Tübingen, 1962),
pp. 51–70.   [14] E. Fraenkel, *op. cit.*, pp. 180 ff. ("Authority as a trust").
[15] Cf. U. Scheuner, "Das repräsentative Prinzip in der modernen Demokratie", *Verfassungsrecht und Verfassungswirklichkeit. Festschrift für
Hans Huber* (Berne, 1961), pp. 222–46. See further Hennis. *loc. cit.*

This basic principle in itself has a decisive influence upon the whole Western tradition of political theory, from the Greek classics to the German theory of kingship and beyond this to the juridical maxim of the Romans, *"Quod omnes tangit ab omnibus approbetur"*. And in fact its influence prevails even where ideas are not conditioned by left-wing strivings against every kind of inequality. What is in question here is not at all the abolishing of the ruling classes in favour of collective self-government on the part of the people, but rather the obligations and responsibilities which power entails.

The comparison with the concept of isonomia and with the interpretation of democracy evolved in the nomistic epoch of the *polis* suggests itself. The title "democracy" can be used to cover this tradition too. It too rejects absolutism, takes freedom as its starting-point and exercises a critical function in relation to government. It is true that prior to modern times the principle of the consensus of the people remains in the background, while the idea of full self-determination comes to the fore, to the extent that it demands merely that the ruled shall have the suffrage (or merely that they shall be accorded a hearing). Nevertheless in the 17th century this is radicalized into the postulate that the rulers shall be totally dependent on the continuing confidence of the ruled, in other words into the basic principle of "representative government".

On the other side the ideas of radical democracy took over that of parliamentary representation because in any case it seemed impossible to have any immediate democracy in the modern state with the vast areas which it covers and the masses which it includes. Thus certain amalgamations of the two traditions were arrived at so that, for instance, Abraham Lincoln identifies the democratic republican regime with the idea of "government of the people by the people and for the people". At the same time there is a constant tension between the two constituent elements of this: the idea of representative government on the one hand and of plebiscitary government on the other; and this has the effect of giving a constantly renewed relevance to the question of the "true" meaning of democracy.[16]

[16] Cf. E. Fraenkel, *Die repräsentative und die plebiszitäre Komponente im demokratischen Verfassungsstaat* (Tübingen, 1958).

III. The Modern Understanding of Democracy

The basic principles of constitutional democracy of the Western type, therefore, are as follows: the self-determination of the people according to the will of the majority as exercised at any given time in freedom and equality. In this all arbitrary forms of government are excluded by the fact that the government in power has to answer for its actions to the people, by the administrators having to conform to the law, by the independence of the judiciary, and in particular by certain basic rights being assured as well as by guaranteeing that the political parties shall have freedom, start on equal terms, and have equality of opportunity. At the same time it must be ensured that all members of the community shall be able to have a say in the policies that are formulated, as well as the best possible chance of the citizens actively collaborating in political life.[17]

In this way it is sought to make "government of the people" possible—government, that is, in the name of the people and by those who are answerable to them, as well as "government for the people", a system of politics designed to uphold the common weal. In all this, however, "government by the people" is intended only indirectly. Radical political self-determination considered as the identification of rulers with ruled as postulated by the original *"polis"* democracy, can in all cases play its part as a controlling idea. The central point in the Western debate on democracy, therefore, is whether this is an absolute necessity and not, after all, merely a virtue.

Rousseau's presentation of the problem is perhaps the clearest: all self-determination in the community presupposes that consent has been achieved in all essential matters in public life. Otherwise, even though decisions may be arrived at on the part of the majority, the minority will feel that they are being subjected to decisions in which they have no voice, and the more important the particular matter involved may be the more intensely they will feel this. Thus Rousseau regards collective self-determination as possible merely in a miniature state and on condition that

---

[17] What the writer has in mind in this statement is a paraphrase of the "basic order of democratic freedom" produced by the Constitutional Court of the Federal Republic of Germany (a judgment of 23 October 1952).

there is homogeneity among the citizens on the social, economic and intellectual levels. At the same time he does consider that, basically speaking, democracy would be suitable only for a population of gods.

This implies that his attitude towards the hope of other thinkers of the 18th century that an identity of will in political matters could be brought to reality is one of resignation. These others had argued that once all irrational traditions and immaturities had been done away with, everyone would come, in virtue of his own natural intelligence, to recognize what best conformed to the common good; that an open and rational critical discussion would lead to findings which carried universal conviction, and would thereby ensure that all would be of the same mind and will in their political orientation.

This theory was founded on the principle that the human conception of reality is rooted in a certain basic intelligence, a law of intelligibility which is objectively recognizable, in other words the application of a rational law of nature. The intellectual homogeneity of the citizens expresses itself in the recognition of this. But this is precisely what now became questionable, even apart from the fact that the basic anthropology which purported to define how social attitudes in the concrete would affect political awareness proved inaccurate. In any case the problem of homogeneity and uniformity of consent was oversimplified. But it is homogeneity that provides the basis for consent that is free from any kind of coercion, and where this homogeneity is not present the achievement of democracy in the radical sense must be problematical. Where differences and a plurality of attitudes and opinions not only exist *de facto*, but are actually asserted, such a democracy must appear positively questionable.

Basically speaking, two ways of escaping from this dilemma present themselves. Either we must modify the conception of democracy in such a way that it does justice to these differences of attitude and outlook and this plurality of opinions, or we must take democracy and democratization actually to mean that overcoming of such plurality and differences in which a full self-determination common to all is made possible.

With regard to the first approach the age yielded a whole

series of suggestions.[18] In the 19th century John Stuart Mill's interpretation of representative democracy acquired great importance. There are discrepancies of interest. In order that the majority shall not impose its interests regardless of those of others the competence of the state must first be restricted by certain norms of liberal justice. Second, political decisions are to be subjected to the principle of reason. Conflicts must be decided conscientiously. Those responsible for carrying out decisions and answerable to the people for this must be characterized by special qualities of integrity. The common interest as generally understood can best be defined by those who are foremost in intelligence and probity. Democracy is, as it were, concentrated in an aristocracy, and thereby the principle of representation is to be given the best chance of succeeding in arriving at political decisions which are right and acceptable. The basic thought here stands in the classical tradition of Western thought from Aristotle onwards.

In an age in which great popular parties appeared Mill's concept gave the impression of being too strongly bound up with a static interpretation of political order. More recent theories have sought to do justice to the dynamic element in the life of party politics. Richard Thoma characterized democracy as government by a particular group as a result of having won an election contest,[19] and a few years later this view was to a large extent reflected in Joseph Schumpeter's theory to the effect that democracy is "that arrangement of institutions for the purpose of arriving at political decisions in which certain individuals win the authority to take decisions by means of a contest with other rival parties for the votes of the people".[20] Several political groups, each with its own programme, compete with one another for the leadership. And in virtue of having to fight for the maximum number of votes they are compelled to "offer" a political programme which is in conformity with the interests of the electorate.

[18] On what follows cf. H. Schneider, "Demokratieverständnis im Widerstreit", *Wissenschaft und Weltbild* 22 (1970), pp. 81 ff.

[19] Cf. R. Thoma, "Der Begriff der modernen Demokratie in seinem Verhältnis zum Staatsbegriff", *Die Hauptprobleme der Soziologie. Erinnerungsgabe für Max Weber* II (Munich, 1923), pp. 39–64.

[20] J. A. Schumpeter, *Capitalism, Socialism and Democracy* (New York, 1942).

Thus democracy is interpreted according to the pattern of the market place. The fact that it is the people, ultimately speaking, who decide is represented as the outcome of a process which automatically "allows the customer to be king" by setting the vendors in competition with one another. If the majority is biased in their way of governing, this can be corrected by the fact that dissatisfaction leads to a different distribution of votes at the next election. In a two-party system each party must, moreover, try to win votes away from the other. As a consequence there is a tendency for both to incline towards the centre in the policies they formulate, and the election contest has a checking and controlling function in that the party in power for the time being has to defend its actions before the eyes of the people against the alternative group (which may, perhaps, be in power in the future and can then be checked and controlled by the group in power at present).

A third basic pattern for constitutional democracy in addition to that of class representation (Mill) and that of dynamic competition (Thoma, Schumpeter, Anthony Downs[21]) is based on the idea of dividing the decisive influence in politics between the representatives of particular social interests according to their relative power in each case, this being determined by the degree of support which they find among the people. The point of departure for this markedly pluralistic conception is not the idea that so long as some political forces are actually ruling others must find themselves in the position of waiting. The idea of a contest in which, at any given time, only some have "arrived" while others are "still on the way" is replaced, as it were, by that of a coalition in which both parties combine as partners. On the basis of this a compromise is arrived at between the various political interests which have been formulated, and thus parties are brought as far as possible (it may be only to a limited extent) to a common agreement. Instead of the will of the community as a homogeneous whole being represented by the will of the particular party which has emerged victorious for the time being in the last election, this will is represented by the results of the various political and social forces having been brought into co-ordination. Those vested with public authority have to follow

[21] A. Downs, *An Economic Theory of Democracy* (New York, 1957).

these results precisely, or at all events in circumstances of doubt to act as arbitrators in deciding what part the jurisdictional authority vested in them is to play in the particular case concerned.

This conception of partnership in a pluralistic society has played an important part in American thought in particular, because there the total community of the citizens has, right from the first, been divided into heterogeneous groups from the ethnical, religious, regional and economic aspects, and because this is the way in which these groups have been able to achieve the recognition which is their due, and at the same time to be fruitfully integrated into the political life.[22] But this is also the pattern to which the "proportional democracies" of Switzerland and Austria (at the time of the Great Coalition) conformed. Furthermore, it seems to a large extent to underly the contemporary expressions of the social teaching of the Catholic Church, as appears in particular from an analysis of the pastoral constitution *Gaudium et spes*.[23]

IV. Current Criticism from the "New Left"

For some time—since the watchwords of democratic reform and democratization have captured the public attention—precisely these conceptions and interpretations of democracy have been exposed to growing criticism.

The pattern of representation by a specific class is considered as being *de facto* a veiled form of oligarchy. If the qualifications of a particular group of citizens for government are upheld, it is said, we cannot speak of democracy in any true sense. The references to the more than average qualities of the rulers are, when they do not constitute a naïve ideology or pure cynicism, an indication, rather, of an underlying structure of society which

[22] R. P. Wolff, "Jenseits der Toleranz", *Kritik der reinen Toleranz*, ed. by Wolff, Moore and Marcuse (Frankfurt, 1966), pp. 9–29.
[23] On Austria and Switzerland cf. G. Lehmbruch, *Proporzdemokratie* (Tübingen, 1967). On the Pastoral Constitution cf. *Die Kirche in der Welt von Heute*, German edition by V. Schurr (Salzburg, 1967), pp. 367–420. For criticisms of this cf. Hans Barion, "Weltgeschichtliche Machtform? Eine Studie zur Politischen Theologie des II. Vatikanischen Konzils", *Epirrhosis, Festgabe für Carl Schmitt* (Berlin, 1968), pp. 13–59.

in truth actually hinders democracy, and in particular of a system of education which promotes oligarchic forms of government. Conditions are such as to make it easy for some to develop their positions but difficult for others. Furthermore, the absolute way in which the protagonists of this theory refer to intellectual and moral qualities and to education in general in itself suggests that standards are being applied which pertain to a quite specific intellectual position and one which is surely more undemocratic than otherwise (because orientated towards tradition).

The pattern in which opposing parties compete with one another is objected to on the grounds that the market only "makes the customer king" in conditions of a fully open competition, whereas the party system in the political pattern which is analogous to this represents an "oligopolis". The representatives of this "oligopolis" are often neither willing nor capable of adapting themselves to the wishes of those who have demands to make, and where the "oligopolis" situation prevails it is only too easy for the formation of pernicious cartels to follow. The basic principles which the theory presupposes are also criticized. Is not this interpretation of politics as a market of competing interests not supported by basic assumptions which are questionable and utilitarian in character? Does it do justice to the real nature of politics if we regard it as a kind of professional service, and here too has not *homo oeconomicus* the citizen arrived, all unreflectingly, at predetermined judgments influenced by subjective categories?

The pluralist model meets with similar objections. It gives the impression of being a cartel of individuals with authority to govern. The chief reason for this is that there is no real equality of opportunity for the social interests involved, the more so since justice in according opportunities must take into account the varying claims of the interests concerned to be legitimate. In fact organized groups within the state who have already carved out a position of power for themselves constantly have an advantage over newly formed ones. *De facto* positions of power in the community are tacitly legitimated. The more rapidly a society transforms itself the more the distortions proliferate which this implies. But on this showing concerns which are different in kind have a very different opportunity of becoming politically effective.

It is easy for the interests of the consumers constantly to be torn apart in the strife between employers and workers. Theoretical interests can hardly be made the concern of particular groups which are ready and capable of expressing themselves in forms of political pressure. And the less these interests are those of specific groups, the more they relate to the general common weal, the more this principle applies. Conversely, in the attempt to establish a co-ordinated system of powers and interests in a pluralistic society it can be that the interests of some extremely narrow faction can achieve an extraordinarily strong influence when those who support them or represent them are especially favoured by circumstances arising from the structure of society as a whole, the way it has been organized or from economic conditions. In extreme cases a cartel is formed of the powerful upholders of particular interests which totally excludes groups and interests which are "not desired". Pluralism, therefore, implies that the "common interests of those who are supreme is used . . . to arrive at an agreement between selected groups . . . in order to suppress and confine the many others".[24]

The question is raised of whether, after all, the representative type of democracy—even according to its own premises —is not in some sense already in operation merely when the official channels of mediation between the citizen and the political entity have been given a democratic form. Doubts are raised as to whether in fact there is an inter-party or inter-factional democracy—indeed, in view of certain insights offered by Robert Michels, whether there is any prospect of success in striving against the tendency towards oligarchy present in every effective organization whatsoever.[25]

Finally criticisms of the representative system of democracy are based on two chief objections. First, if we take as our basis a merely formal conception of democracy we shall confine our gaze to the state and shut out society from view. Second, even the institutional organizations of the state itself will not be viewed

---

[24] Kirchheimer, op. cit., p. 93.
[25] Cf. R. Michels, Zur Soziologie des Parteienwesens in der modernen Demokratie (New edition, Stuttgart, 1957). On the recent discussion of the problem cf. F. Naschold, Organisation und Demokratie (Stuttgart, 1969).

from standpoints that are democratic in the true sense. Now if this system of institutions is understood to be an instrument for bringing to the fore accepted representatives of government and for the production of accepted acts of government on the part of these representatives, then from the very outset we are renouncing all attempts to take seriously the original democratic viewpoint in which all are intended to be given the maximum possible chance of active participation in political life, taking this to be a dimension of human self-realization. In other words we shall be shutting out the humanistic perspective which is already present in the Aristotelian political conception, according to which the community must offer each individual the possibility of developing and maintaining in the most favourable circumstances possible his own intelligent and conscientious participation in political life as well. Now we must not renounce the principle of "government by the people" in this sense.

In other words: any solution of the democratic dilemma which seeks to replace the principle of self-determination on the part of a community by the rulers ultimately answerable to that community they represent is accounted as erroneous. What we have here, basically speaking, in place of something that approaches to democracy is a mere appearance of it, an autocratic or oligarchic government covered over with a democratic gloss. The political freedom and equality of the citizens as formally guaranteed by the representative system of democracy extends only to the actual way in which the political institutions themselves function, while at the same time it excludes those prior conditions which are necessary for the citizens to stand in a positive relationship to these institutions. It is only in an imperfect sense that this regime can even be called "government of the people". Prior to the life of the institutions in which such government is officially embodied certain conditions of power and influence may from time to time prevail in a given society, and towards these this sort of regime remains neutral (but even this is to be taken *cum grano salis*, for every institution has a certain affinity to certain specific elements in the area which it covers, and hence acts as a filter in relation to these).

It is necessary to alter the social substructure of the community inasmuch as conditions which militate radically against freedom and equality have played their part in shaping this. Otherwise even that condition which is ascribed to the representative system, according to which the government is checked and controlled by the people (to say nothing of government by the people) fails to function. For instance if the mass media of communication are, to an overwhelming extent, under the control of those who uphold particular interests, then these determine to a large extent what problems are to be raised at all, and so what political judgments are to be formed.

Thus the left wing regards the destruction of such positions of ascendancy in society as a necessary prior condition for true constitutional democracy to introduce its own distinctive determinations. Likewise the doing away with privileges and positions of power signifies for democracy in this true sense that emancipation of classes which have hitherto been underprivileged and which in the end will do away with basic oppositions of interest within the society (class divisions) to such an extent that the democratic dilemma will be totally overcome. For then majority decisions will no longer signify any kind of dictatorship on the part of one section of society over another, and only then can the community as a whole think with one mind. In accordance with this, and after the distortions in the shape of society which already corrupt representative democracy have been overcome, the idea which is characteristic of radical democracy of full self-determination on the part of all will once more become actual: a form of political government which is truly answerable to the will of the people, yet at the same time distinct from it, appears possible only at that stage at which it is no longer necessary at all.[26]

Thus according to the ideal pattern of democracy which they have created, the representatives of the left wing foresee not only "social democratization" but also a transformation of the specifically political institutions. With regard to this latter the "council"

[26] A point for consideration in this connection is how often the concept of government is applied unreflectingly, as also is the idea that once economic equality with regard to the means of production has been achieved there would be no more conflicts which would require governmental control. On this cf. H. Schneider, *loc. cit.*, "Conclusion". A well-thought-out interpretation in a different sense is to be found in Narr, *loc. cit.*

pattern of government often plays a major role.[27] The members of the community assemble in primary groups defined by the area in which they dwell, or—as a primary factor—by their calling. All political problems are, as far as possible, discussed and decided at this level. Community tasks which cannot be catered for by these primary groups themselves are, in accordance with a strict principle of delegation, entrusted to mandatories who are directly chosen, who constantly have to account for their actions to the electors involved and can be deposed at any moment. All such mandates are honorary, or else any emoluments they carry are tied to the level of the average income in the community. Committees existing at higher levels (councils directly elected at particular times) are intended as far as possible faithfully to reflect the social structure of the community of electors. Frequent re-election is forbidden. There is a rotation of official functions which is intended to give as many as possible an active share in politics. It seems superfluous, if not positively harmful, to seek to escape from power. All this is intended to prevent institutions which are meant to be representative from becoming autonomous, and to counter any tendencies towards oligarchy and bureaucracy.

At the same time certain growing difficulties would have to be reckoned with which are, of their nature, prejudicial to the functioning of a *"polis"* democracy. A division of political tasks which is as far as possible equable requires that all shall constantly be ready to engage in such tasks, and that they shall have an unusual degree of political education. The modern society has a far greater need of supra-regional organization and co-ordination than any former one, to say nothing of the *polis* itself. To seek constantly to bring decisions down to the judgment and decision-making of the primary groups would imply restricting to a dangerous extent the practical capability of the system for planning and taking decisions (at least with regard to the time necessary for this). The very fact that providing the members of the primary groups with the information required for rational decisions costs time and money is in itself enough to show this, quite apart from the fact that the danger of being selective in the

[27] Cf. P. von Oertzen, *Betriebsräte in der Novemberrevolution* (Düsseldorf, 1963); E. Ertl, *Alle Macht den Räten?* (Frankfurt, 1968).

information provided—in other words of the manipulation of the public awareness from above—would again make it necessary to devise precautions against this.

Thus it is hardly an accident that up to the present councils have played important parts only in revolutions, when those concerned were in any case fully involved, and when the very situation itself made it fairly clear what political measures had to be taken. By contrast attempts at setting up purely political councils in "post-revolutionary" situations have constantly proved failures.[28] Admittedly another question which may seriously be raised is whether the conception of the council does not after all offer certain elements entailed in the process of giving active force to the idea of democracy which might also be applied in different circumstances. An instance of this would be the idea of federal membership (though admittedly in this regard such "subsystems" of political participation would have to guard against falling into the role of mere channels of communication by which the will of the governing power was transmitted from above).

Certainly there are signs that the traditional system of Western democracy is capable of being modified both theoretically and structurally by institutional developments which increase the opportunities for participation in social and political decision-making (from the lowering of the age of suffrage to the voting regulations in various spheres of public life). This traditional system can also be modified in the sense of allowing fresh levels of significance to be opened up in it. To give a few examples of this we may cite the adopting of the principle of human self-realization through political activity in conceptions of democracy to which such ideas did not formally come so naturally, or the effort to enrich the formal pattern of electional contests in democracy by the factor of movements for social emancipation. As representative of the first perspective we can point, for instance, to the thesis of Hermann Josef Wallraffs to the effect that democracy is not only an institutional means for furthering the common weal, but an integral element in the common weal

[28] Cf. U. Bermbach, "Ansätze zu einer Kritik des Rätesystems", *Berliner Zeitschrift für Politologie* 9 (1968), Section 4, pp. 21–31.

itself. An instance of the second perspective would be Dahrendorf's conception of a social liberal democracy ("the machinery for regulating social conflicts at the political level with the aim of achieving a controlleed change of society").[29]

V. The Understanding of Democracy in the East and among the Developing Nations

It is necessary to distinguish what is called democracy in the "socialist camp" and in the "third world" from the theory of democracy characteristic of the "Western left" as described above. It is true that in the socialist camp and the third world too the traditional Western systems are interpreted as veiled dictatorships on the part of those who already have power. The characteristic of the communist-orientated systems—including their claim to be counted as democratic—is, however, connected with certain specific developments in the Marxist doctrine. To Marxism[30] it appeared justifiable to equate true democracy with dictatorship of the proletariat. Yet it interprets democracy in a "kratistic" sense as government by the majority in favour of their own specific interests so that it is presupposed here that it is in any case possible for the proletariat to take over power only if it includes the overwhelming majority of the population as a whole. The taking over of power by the working class, however, appears to its champions not only formally (as majority government) but even more in terms of content as a democratic event to the extent that it is a prior condition for setting up a classless society and thereby one that makes radical democracy possible.

A crisis arose over these ideas when precisely in industrially developed societies the working class which had grown up were far from taking over the role which had been foreseen for them of becoming the revolutionary proletariat. Lenin[31] concluded that the revolution must be brought about by a disciplined skeleton organization, in other words by the "party" deliberately acting as an *avant-garde* for the seizing of power by the proletariat. In

[29] For references cf. H. Schneider, *loc. cit.*
[30] Cf., for instance, H. Kelsen, *Sozialismus und Staat* (Vienna, 1965[3])
[31] Cf., for instance, H. J. Lieber and K. H. Ruffmann, *Der Sowjetkommunismus* I–II (Cologne, 1963).

a nation which was socially and economically so backward that it made any idea of revolution by a proletarian majority seem absurd, the rule of the party founded by Lenin became a crude dictatorship of development which sought thereby to create a basis for itself on which to build in later generations in the future.

The basic historical ideology which the communists were following envisaged a progress of mankind which was as beneficial as it was necessary, according to the laws of the system, in order for it to become a uniquely human, because classless, society (and thereby capable of spontaneous common self-determination). In view of this, therefore, the communists sought to appease their democratic consciences by interpreting the autocratic mode of government which they had set up as a necessary means of achieving the aim of democracy in the true sense: the development of productivity in order to overcome the scarcity of materials and at the same time the development of awareness and the accustoming of attitudes to universal solidarity demanded the most extreme co-ordination of resources and the suppressing of liberalism as too costly. Lenin was perfectly well aware of the character of his party's dictatorship as imposing discipline by force. But he maintained that such a "forced cure" was indispensable in a society which had been corrupted by centuries of exploitation, quite apart from the necessity of industrialization which literally means "causing to be industrious", in other words the mobilization of men for a productivity programme which was to grow as steeply as possible.

In spite of this he did regard it as possible to introduce elements of democratic forms of government into the party system. The leaders were intended to institute a "democratic centralism" by a process of election from the ranks, in which all political problems as they appeared could be freely and comprehensively discussed. After the conclusion had been arrived at the decision was, admittedly, intended to be totally binding, and every member was obliged to work actively for it to be carried out. Lenin sought to allow discussion within the party because he supposed that in a "cadre" party with a clear ideology all would, in any case, identify themselves with the ultimate definitive aims, so that differences of opinion would relate only to methods and tactics, and hence no one would have his conscience forced by the decisions arrived at. However, this proved to be an over-optimistic estimate for the very reason that in politics means and aims, the goal and the way to it, strategy and tactics, are not capable of being determined independently of one another.

The politics of Stalin seemed to be determined by a restricted horizon of thought and action designed to secure and increase the power of the party and of its instruments of government. All that was left of Lenin's concept was, so to say, the bureaucratic centralizing of direction. In the post-Stalin era there are, nevertheless, signs that the centres of political control take the *de facto* interests of the citizens more strongly into account than was formerly the case. How far this can be called "democratization", where it can lead and how far it will go—these are, admittedly, questions which could be the subject of a thesis in itself.

A further point is that in forming its views the Eastern world has not simply taken over the Soviet system piecemeal. One expression of this has been the development of the concept of the "People's democracy" (a term which has a somewhat discordant ring to Western ears). This differs from the "dictatorship of the proletariat" in that in it it is a "coalition of progressive forces" that carries on the government, albeit as subject to a proletarian "hegemony". The "People's democracy" idea has come, so to say, to stand for a further development—indeed for an overthrowing of the formal type of democracy (considered as government by the property-owning citizens), while still not amounting to government purely by the plebeian Demos. Rather it is a transitional measure in which the working class has not suppressed certain other still notable groups, but has been given a share in the government. The reason for this is that the transfer of power has met with far less opposition than in Russia, and hence the subsequent "intensification of the class struggle" has seemed unnecessary.[32] "People's democracy" signifies a regime, therefore, in which the demos in the broader sense governs under the direction of the demos in the narrower sense.

In Yugoslavia a more far-reaching development was achieved in the process of time in that party government was made open

[32] Cf. Z. K. Brzezinski, *Der Sowjetblock* (Cologne, 1962), pp. 43–53, 66–72.

3—C.

to a greater extent to functional elements of democracy in the form of initiatives for the self-direction of industry and local government. These were sponsored by the idea of the democratic council.

The conceptions of democracy signified by the expression "third world" bear a different stamp. The pre-industrial forms of life, differing from culture to culture, provide a basis (it could contain certain basic structural factors of governmental forms and social groupings as well as habits of thought[33]) on which, as a result of taking over the product of alien cultures (ranging from techniques of production to intellectual approaches), a profound and far-reaching transformation takes place, and one which throws the traditional orderings of social life and systems of government into a crisis. The need for public service grows rapidly. The chief area of concern is the developments taking place within the existing framework, such as the conclusion of trade agreements and the emergence of the educated element, the development of a social policy and similar factors.

Since those involved cannot attach themselves to liberal traditions as in the West, the system of competitive democracy, despite the fact that it provides an apt mode in which to express the dynamic elements in the life of society, has little chance of establishing itself. The very fact that the range of alternatives which are available to the population to choose from in arriving at a rational decision is a narrow one is, of itself, enough to make this true. And there is the further factor that the very abundance and importance of the tasks of development call for a strong leadership and a concentration of all forces. This means that there is hardly any appreciation of the need for a permanent and institutionalized opposition. Thus frequently one-party regimes emerge with ideologies which correspond to the ideas of Rousseau: the expression of a *"volonté générale"* appears to be a necessary requirement of the national development which, in fact, often includes as a preliminary the overcoming of extremist orientations on the part of particular factions. (These are bound

[33] Cf., for instance, R. Behrendt, *Soziale Strategie für Entwicklungsländer* (Frankfurt, 1965). For an enlightening account of the mentality involved (for Asia), E. Skrisyanz, *Russland und der Massianismus des Orients* (Tübingen, 1955).

up with family, tribal and regional divisions). Quite apart from the overcoming of traditionalism in general, therefore, these too have to be overcome.

Political self-awareness acquires a special and peculiar emphasis in those cases in which political independence has been won only by means of great struggles or through revolutionary action, and in which, in the face of continuing economic dependence, in various respects, anti-colonialist views are disseminated, so that Marxist ideas are echoed in the sense of a class struggle on the part of the peoples. In such cases democracy signifies the taking over of power on the part of those who have been exploited, in the sense that the people as a whole deprive the former colonial rulers of their power. "Interior" class oppositions are, by comparison, less explosive—so long as elements among the rulers do not make common cause with the "colonialists". In any case, for the most part anti-colonialism is a more far-reaching motive force for the expression or manipulation of a *volonté générale*, and one which runs parallel to the drive for social mobilization (for the sake of building up modern systems of production) and to the compelling need for the swift integration of the new nation. All these factors tell in favour of conceptions of democracy which owe nothing to the liberal tradition of the West, but in spite of revolutionary traits they also exhibit essential differences from Marxism and Leninism.

What is common to both is, as a rule, the basic idea that by means of common strivings on the part of all the people solidly united, a civilizational and political basis must be created in order that the human capabilities of all members of the community may be realized fully and freely. But ultimately speaking all the theories and ideologies of democracy which belong to the new age are brought into harmony with this ultimate goal, and, therefore, with the "humanism" inherent in the basic intention.

VI. The Future of Democracy

In our time there are only a few regimes and only a few adherents still left of any schools of thought which represent a radical alternative to democracy, in whatever sense they differ from it. Even military regimes justify themselves on the grounds that the transitional disciplining of the people is salutary as a prior condition to the formation of "genuine" democracy. Greece is not the only example of the fact that autocrats pay at least a verbal tribute to democracy.

The tendency to cast doubts upon non-democratic political forms is therefore world-wide. But is it merely some kind of fashion in world history? There is much that tells against this view. Ever since Karl Mannheim sociologists have pointed to that "basic impulse to democracy"[34] the world-wide character of which is becoming ever clearer. The basis of this is an all-embracing and gradual process which Max Weber has depicted as "a general rationalization of existence". The conditions of life become capable of alteration. What was earlier accounted as the natural order was stabilized by tradition and set apart from the areas subject to active human control. But today this has become material for man to use and shape to his requirements, and this applies to the sphere in which natural resources are subjected to technical manipulation as well as to the social and cultural aspects of human life. This does not necessarily represent an advance or an improvement, but it is a measure of how far and how deeply men have had to assume added responsibility for the realities involved in their own lives and of how this responsibility is still increasing. Meanwhile this same transformation depends upon an increasing division of functions and a more and more complex division of tasks and services, as well as a greater degree of integration between them. At the same time the mutual interdependence between the individual and the collective group is intensified. This means that the individual in particular cannot give due attention to the responsibility that needs to be taken. At the same time this responsibility can hardly be left to anonymous civil servants to discharge. It is primarily the affair of the body politic, and this means that human life must become political through and through.

At the same time the tempo of social change renders necessary a continual process of increase and change in the acquisition of knowledge in modern society. The individual in it is, so to say, in

[34] K. Mannheim, *Mensch und Gesellschaft im Zeitalter des Umbaus* (1935, new and revised edition Darmstadt, 1958), pp. 52 ff. (*Man and Society in the Age of Reconstruction*, London, 1940).

no position to adopt an attitude of mere passive submissiveness and so to allow events to pass over him. The ways in which society functions require an active participation and a rational orientation on his part (which imposes extraordinary demands upon the individual, so that in face of them it may be more natural to capitulate by blinding oneself to the broader issues involved by having recourse to narcotics, etc.).

All these factors taken together should gradually bring about an advance in social and political awareness leading in the direction of democracy, especially when the increase in social productivity in an industrial society paves the way for the sort of far-reaching liberation from toil and for those opportunities of education which permit all to play their part in politics (this is in contrast to the age of the *polis*). To an increasing extent the state of being embedded in traditions which are never called in question gives way to the expression of interests, to discussions and rival claims for votes. Certainly this goes hand in hand with an increase in literacy and urbanization. At the turn of the century only a very small percentage of the total human population lived in cities. By the middle of the century every fifth man did so. Today it is already every third man. By 1955 the fifty per cent threshold in the ability to read and write—in earlier epochs this was a privilege reserved to small minorities—was surpassed on a world-wide scale.[35] Yet such processes are not restricted to the urban modes of life (to cite an immediately relevant example, farmers are noticing more and more that the earnings of agriculture can become a factor in politics).

Wherever it is no longer the case that the development of political awareness is confined to a minority in society, it is becoming increasingly difficult, if not actually impossible, to maintain a heterogeneous form of government in which different classes are subject to different laws. Where such forms of government exist they need, to say the least, to develop more advanced techniques of manipulation. For in former times it was possible totally to eliminate opposition movements, which in any case comprised only one section of the politically aware minority, without any danger to the continuing existence and functioning

[35] K. Deutsch, "The Future of World Politics", *Political Quarterly* I (1966).

of society as a whole. Now, however, this is no longer *ipso facto* possible. The degree of complexity and the need for efficiency in the society of today and tomorrow absolutely demands systems of control which are sensitive and responsive to the requirements of the controlled, in other words for institutions to be set up for mutual intercommunication between those exercising functions affecting wide sections of the population, and those affected by such tasks. The development and carrying through of forms of association which are democratic, or at least show tendencies towards democracy, seem to have a positively predestined character. Policy-makers consciously extend their range of vision so as to cover whole centuries,[36] though it is true that this does not mean that their policies are to be regarded as any kind of historical automatism. What it does mean, surely, is that their increased vision has to be recognized as inspiring tendencies which are more penetrating in their effect.

VII. DEMOCRACY AND CHRISTIANITY

Up to this point the spiritual foundations of modern democracy have been left out of the discussion. Among these mention must be made of Christianity. Admittedly democracy and Christianity have rarely been regarded as so closely interrelated as they were in the time of Cromwell, when democracy was said absolutely to be "a religious and moral principle" and "the translation of the universal priesthood into non-theological language".[37] The question arises whether what we are dealing with here is a specific ideology—in other words a false kind of awareness: whether, or to what extent, what is being expressed is, as it were, the distinctive body of ideas belonging to one particular area of history, with its own political philosophy and its own confessional tenets: or alternatively whether, and to what extent, it is the case that here a close relationship between Christianity and democracy in general is being given a particularly pregnant embodiment. If there is such a close interrelationship it may be

[36] A. de Tocqueville, *De la Démocratie en Amérique* I–III (Paris, 1835–1840). For the contemporary viewpoint cf. K. Deutsch, *The Nerves of Government* (New York, 1966²).
[37] According to G. Leibholz, *Das Wesen der Repräsentation und der Gestaltwandel der Demokratie im 20. Jahrhundert* (Berlin, 1966³), p. 211.

due either to the derivation of democracy from Christianity or alternatively to the fact that both have special structural affinities.

It is possible to assemble a whole range of statements in favour of such an interconnection between the two—perhaps less in the sense of a direct preaching or legitimizing of democratic principles of government, and more in the sense of a laying down of principles or a demanding of views which can more or less open the way to democracy, make it easier to justify, or even adduce, fresh motives for introducing it. Over and above this, in many cases we can also point to indications of the fact that this interconnection has been effective in history at the social and political level. The Old Testament[38] introduces the prototype of the *theopoliteia*. "All the sons of Israel belong directly (*kohanim* in its original meaning) to the Lord."[39] Earthly monarchy appears as a compromise with requirements to which the environmental factors of the time gave rise, and to have rather been conceded than willed by the Lord (1 Sam.). The prophetic movement shows that even under the monarchy the life of the community was not subject to human rule alone. In the prophetic preaching the criticisms of exploitation and oppression, of unjust forms of government and discriminating between classes in the administration of justice, are too strong to be ignored.

The New Testament proclaims the inversion of the "natural" political picture for the world. He who bears a responsibility for others must act as their servant. He who will be the first must be the last. No one may let himself be called master, father or teacher. Even if we may, as we surely must, understand Jesus' message, and still more the preaching of the early community, as a "blueprint" for a *theopoliteia*, the basic composition of which was of a radical-democratic character, still again and again it was the eschatological orientation that first prompted individuals or groups to set the "kingdom of God" ideal as their direct political

[38] On the significance of the Old Testament for political thinking in the Anglo-Saxon sphere cf. H. Schöffler, *Wirkungen der Reformation—Religionssoziologische Folgerungen für England und Deutschland* (Frankfurt, 1960).

[39] Cf., for instance, H. Berkhof, *Kirche und Kaiser* (Zollikon–Zurich, 1947); F. Kern, *Gottesgnadentum und Widerstandsrecht im frühen Mittelalter* (Darmstadt, 1954²); R. Schnur, ed., *Zur Geschichte der Erklärung der Menschenrechte* (Darmstadt, 1964).

goal. Secondly, even in those cases in which the tension between the inauguration and the final fulfilment of the kingdom of God was accepted in faith, the preaching of the Gospel could be, and indeed had to be, understood as a summons to live as disciples of Jesus, and consequently potential political motives are latent in it for all ages (or are more and more so). And these motives have been able to be worked out in democratic forms of life and government. Thirdly, this applies surely in a quite special sense to that sphere of life which is constituted as a representation of the kingdom of God already existing in the age of expectation: to the Church. In her history constant fresh efforts can be discerned to bring about a renewal of the spirit of free evangelical brotherhood, to withdraw from the political forms and styles of government belonging to a particular time, which had become the standards by which the Church herself was ruled.

In this connection the founding of the great orders likewise deserves attention, as also do the efforts at reform initiated by the councils at the beginning of the new age. But we should also notice those groups which broke away from the Church, the sects of the free spirit of the early Middle Ages from Wyclif and Hus to the Quakers, and similar manifestations of a still later age. The Reformation doctrine of the priesthood of all believers is particularly noteworthy here as the basis for the Congregationalist image of the Church. But a fourth effect was brought about precisely by that attitude of eschatological reserve in accordance with which Christians as citizens of the "kingdom of heaven" put their commonwealth or *politeuma* before all the responsibilities they owed as citizens or subjects of the political powers of this world. This brings about a change in politics in general. It comes to be regarded as not the ultimate factor in all cases.

This has far-reaching consequences. Duties towards God provide a basis for inalienable rights which human powers owe to the individual. From the Church's struggles for her own constitutional status in the Roman empire to the political ethics of the Middle Ages and from this right down to the modern idea of freedom of religious conscience and the expression of this in legal statutes (the origin of the human rights of modern times!), there develops from this point onwards an ultimate dimension of political freedom. This in turn implies the recognition of a dimension of existence which is metapolitical, and which provides an ultimate standard, so that now the political reality belonging to this world is divested of any sacral unassailability and can become an object which men can transform and reshape afresh according to their own freely thought-out ideas (however long they may have to wait before this is fully accomplished in human history). It is precisely this that has made it possible for the sphere of social organization to become, in a radical sense, an area in which human freedom and intelligence can achieve developments—probably anything similar to this was only possible in the *polis*. In contrast to the *sacra regna* and *imperia*, "civil government" becomes possible as a specifically human activity.

All this should be borne in mind when we come to consider the modern understanding of democracy. Yet on the other hand outstanding minds have come forward again and again, first Eusebius of Caesarea, then Pseudo-Dionysius, then Dante, Bossuet and, still later, right down to Donoso Cortes, whose expressed views make it seem as though there were an unbridgeable gulf between the Christian and the democratic outlook. Yet in relatively recent times, in treating of the interior structure of the Catholic Church, Clemens Bauer could make the following pronouncement: "From the end of antiquity onwards the Church absorbs all forms of political constitution into the organic structure of her own interior institutions, whether to imitate them or to transform them. The constitutional mode of the state organized on liberal and democratic lines is something that she cannot assimilate or imitate, or rather it is not reconcilable with her own interior nature and the basic principles of her organization."[40]

Can it be, therefore, that the discussion of democratization is utterly meaningless? Or does it admit of any revision or modification of opinions such as those we have cited—modifications which would tend to suggest that the Church is, as it were, constantly exposed to influences from her environment and from contemporary society even in respect of her innermost organization and even in the age of democracy? In that case it would be a demand of this present hour that we should inquire of the secular understanding of democracy what it has to offer to the

[40] C. Bauer, "Bild der Kirche—Abbild der Gesellschaft", *Hochland* 48 (1955/56), pp. 519–27, esp. 526.

Ecclesia semper reformanda with regard to her structural organization.

Admittedly it would not be so easy to find any basis for holding that there is a *fundamental* affinity—as distinct from one which arises merely from the conditions of a particular epoch—between Christian and democratic thought. But perhaps there is another way. Is it not the case that Christianity's understanding of itself on the one hand, and the world's understanding of itself on the other, provide thought-forms and categories of meaning which include fresh dimensions in which the legitimacy of "democracy" and "democratization" can be recognized, without thereby *ipso facto* giving expression to the actual "content" of democratic doctrines?[41] The interpretation of existence implicit in Christian faith and thinking brings home to individuals and societies the idea of personal responsibility and self-determination more intensively than any other interpretation of reality in terms of pre-established categories. At the same time the words and works of Christ himself proclaim the promise of the kingdom of God in which there will be perfect freedom and solidarity, and that too not merely as something which is prophesied for the future but as something that is already present.

Notwithstanding the difficulties involved in controlling the tension to be found here in terms of eschatology and salvation history, this means that an idea is suggested which has relevance to political thought as well, which up to now has never failed to disturb men's imaginations. Helmut Kuhn argues that there is "in all community life" an "*a priori* vision" which "is present as a universally recognized standard, either explicitly or implicitly taken into account even in those cases in which the political opinions come most fiercely and irreconcilably into collision: this is the concept of living together in complete harmony in a community of peace and love".[42] We may suppose that Aristotle's conception of intelligent self-realization in the *polis* can be

[41] On the question of the patterns of thought and on the thesis in general cf. J. B. Metz, *Christliche Anthropozentrik* (Munich, 1962), and also the same author's "Weltverständnis im Glauben", *Geist und Leben* 35 (1962), pp. 165–84

[42] H. Kuhn, "Philosophie—Ideologie—Politik", *Zeitschrift für Politik* 10 (1963), pp. 4–35, esp. p. 17.

included in this idea, as also can Jürgen Habermas's "majority intention" as expressed in "general and unconstrained consent", and in "free communication exempt from direction from above".[43]

Has not Christian thought imparted to this "*a priori* vision" a fresh level of meaningfulness and one which has surpassed all attempts, both earlier and later, to define the essence of the political good, whether it be the theories of the Stoa or Herbert Marcuse's "pacified existence"? Has not Christian thought achieved this because it rises to the ideal of complete freedom and brotherhood in the full participation of all in the rule of God? Augustine's concept of the *civitas caelestis*, for instance, is defined in terms of true *pax*, *concordia* and *libertas* in such a way that, strictly speaking, God does not rule over men, but will be "all in all" (1 Cor. 15. 28). "Dominion" in the specifically modern sense of prevailing over the will of the individual in the interests of another is on this showing precisely ruled out in favour of an idea of self-fulfilment in its most perfect form, one which also infinitely transcends the image of supralapsarian freedom from dominion (according to this man was intended from the beginning to rule over his flocks rather than his fellow men). In this respect, therefore, this idea signifies nothing less than mutual collaboration, in view of the fact that God himself is three in one.

It belongs to our understanding of what it means to be part of salvation history at all to recognize that the force of the eschatological pull inherent in this vision should not lead us simply to turn aside from earthly politics, but rather, despite all the dangers of wrongly restricting its application to the immanent dimension of this present world, should let it inspire us with the ideals of freedom, equality and brotherhood. This level of meaning, together with the way of thinking of divine, human and historical realities that goes with it, gives scope and strength for action whether at the individual or the collective levels, the goals and standards of which—to formulate them in the political language of today— can be called democracy. On this showing the secular conception of democracy would find its basis in the Christian understanding

[43] J. Habermas, *Technik und Wissenschaft als Ideologie* (Frankfurt, 1969).

of reality in general, though admittedly it became aware of this only after a long period of clarification and of maturing the implications and conclusions contained within its own tenets.[44]

VIII. Conclusion

What has been said up to this point is not sufficient to establish clearly what the modern Church's understanding of democracy can signify and can lead to. But surely we can determine a few of the necessary prior conditions for this.

If "democracy" is taken to be the title of a political programme which is directed to full human self-realization in freedom and solidarity, then this basic orientation is rooted in principles which, to say the least, are capable of being made a manifestation of the Christian understanding of God, of the world and of Christianity itself, and therein find a justification and fulfilment which can surely never be surpassed.

In contrast to this, however, "democracy" as used in contemporary political parlance stands for movements and organizations of various kinds. For many "radical democrats" it can stand for a realization, as far as possible direct and uncompromising, of the vision of full common self-determination, and this will be achieved through a more or less forceful abolishment of "the mechanisms of repression". Numbered among these is any kind of institutional organization of human life as such, and the basic presuppositions underlying this attitude spring from anthropological ideas which are crude in the extreme.[45] Here Christians may suspect that even apart from the naturalistic limitations imposed upon man's understanding of himself, all these attempts involve an evasion of the eschatological factor which has constantly to be borne in mind, and they remind themselves that attempts to seize the kingdom of God (or some kind of substitute for this) by force have again and again led to a situation in which force is used against the individual man.

[44] Cf. Metz, op. cit. (1962), pp. 124 ff. ("The new age as the outcome, re-expressed in different categories of thought, of the Thomist and Christian system of ideas.")

[45] Thus, perhaps, H. Marcuse, Triebstruktur und Gesellschaft (Frankfurt, 1965); idem, "Repressive Toleranz", Kritik der reinen Toleranz, ed. by Wolff, Moore and Marcuse (Frankfurt, 1966), pp. 93–128.

On the other hand "democracy" designates various kinds of political organizations which, in their application to the current situation in human living, and the potential for social action which this contains, are offered as, relatively speaking, the best ways of institutionalizing the principle of common self-determination. Various patterns of "democratic" constitutions compete with one another, each being presented as the best "democracy of the possible". In the Western world in particular this is claimed to be the constitutional system of representation, together with the changes and alternations which this involves, even though these are objected to by its critics.

Over and above this there is a linguistic usage in which "democratization" signifies neither the direct establishing of a state based on perfect brotherhood nor yet the setting up of specific constitutional forms designed to ensure that authority to take decisions shall constantly be subject in the best possible way to the authorization and control of those who are being governed. In this system the measures taken to ensure this can in turn relate either to the state alone or to the state and society. But what is intended by the term "democratization" at this level is not this, but rather certain specific intellectual and moral attitudes, in other words an ethos which corresponds to the vision or *eidos* of democracy: mutual respect, a readiness to make the common interest one's own and to listen to one another, a discussion in which all who are affected by a given decision are accorded a hearing, even when this decision is formally laid down by specific authorities who are hardly answerable at all, or only in a marginal sense, to those who are affected by it.[46]

And finally there are certain transitional positions between these three levels of meaning in "democracy". For example, when the demand for discussion (as distinct from collaboration in decision-making) is made a constitutional right, or when institutions are

[46] The well-known study of E. W. Böckenförde, "Das Ethos der modernen Demokratie und die Kirche", *Hochland* 50 (1957/58), pp. 16 ff., focuses almost exclusively upon the model of the market as a pattern for democracy. On the problem of the democratic ethos cf. also H. Schneider, "Rechtsstaatliche Demokratie und politische Bildung", *Erziehungswissenschaftliches Handbuch* I, ed. by Ellwein, Groothoff, Rauschenberger and Roth (Berlin, 1969), pp. 101–37, esp. 112–29.

projected in such a way that *de facto* they lead to a process of interchange which is as broadly based and as full as possible, so that any kind of autonomous representationalism is reduced to a minimum (as in the system of councils). Even when we come to speak of "democracy in the Church" or of the "democratization" of the Church, there are several levels or degrees at which "democratic" movements manifest themselves. The first of these corresponds, in historical terms so to say, to the principle formulated immediately before the modern age of the need for taking counsel and obtaining consent for all official enactments of government. In this connection the status and basis for these official positions, as well as the appointment of those who hold them, is still independent of, and does not fall within the sphere of, collective control. The second level would be that even the setting up of offices and the appointing of the officials themselves would reflect an act of trust and expression of will on the part of the community as a whole. And in practice this means on the part of the majority. The political analogy here would be the modern constitutional state considered as an institution of representative government. A third dimension of "democratization" could only signify the tendency to overcome the vesting of official authority in representatives in general, and the reducing of this to a minimum in practice in favour of the free community of brothers.

The connection is clear. Perhaps the easiest way of indicating it precisely is with the help of certain ideas belonging to the theory of communications which in any case can be translated into current theological ideas. Corresponding to the vision of full and complete common self-determination would be a dialogue that was free, undistorted and open to all. In the actual conditions of our life this would represent an extreme concept, as has been shown precisely by the more recent research into communications.[47] At the other end of the scale we have, so to say, that way of conducting life and taking decisions which is pure monologue —this likewise is an extreme concept. The aims of "democratization" are to give an increasing place to dialogue, and the establishment of an increasing equilibrium in social dialogue. The distortions in this, which are due to inequalities in the social

[47] Cf. F. Naschold, *op. cit.*, p. 30, and also the bibliography supplied there.

organization, are admittedly incapable of ever being completely eliminated.[48]

It is only in the light of distinctions of this kind that we can decide what is desirable and necessary in all this for the Church, even though we are thankful for the fact that at the present moment the Church is coming to terms with democratic ideas and forms to a greater extent than ever.

[48] Cf. J. Habermas, *op. cit.*, and also his *Erkenntnis und Interesse* (Frankfurt, 1968). With regard to the limits of the possibility of rectifying communications it is sufficient to refer to the physical factor. Interesting views on this point are also offered by W. Hennis, *op. cit.* (n. 2), pp. 35 ff.

Translated by David Bourke

Rudolf Pesch

The New Testament Foundations of a Democratic Form of Life in the Church

THE "historical law of the merging together of the Church and society"[1] is expressed today in the call to make the Church more democratic. On the one hand, this need to make the Church democratic becomes more urgent as the conditions governing this law become, as the result of historical and sociological research, more fully understood, not only by specialists, but also by people in general. On the other hand, its validity is also increased as the non-eschatological, unadapted character of the Church's forms of life, official structures and legal forms, which are not adequate any longer to the *kairos* and which have at the same time been very much delayed as far their reform is concerned compared with those in the secular sphere, are subjected to more and more public criticism, most of which is entirely justified.

Where this criticism has not been applied to an "overadapted" Church, in other words, to its levelling out as the "sign of contradiction" indicating direction and extent, it has to be orientated towards the original source and document of the life of the Church, the New Testament, and the basic, "constitutional" law of the Church's form of life contained in it and express itself in the spirit of the New Testament as a "prophetic" criticism.[2]

Are there any foundations of a *democratic* form of life in the Church in the New Testament? We are bound to be on our guard

[1] C. Bauer, *Deutscher Katholizismus. Entwicklungslinien und Profile* (Frankfurt, 1964), p. 27.
[2] See J. Blank, *Das Evangelium als Garantie der Freiheit* (Würzburg, 1970).

at the very outset against the view that the call to make the Church more democratic can be interpreted according to the norm of a basic law of a Church form of life contained in the New Testament as a demand that the rule of the Church should be made democratic, rather along the lines of "the exercise of power in the Church must correspond with the exercise of power in the world, in other words, the way of exercising power in the Church must change as the forms of rule and power in the world change".[3]

Over and against an opinion of this kind, attention must be drawn to a clear saying by Jesus handed down to us as part of the instructions given to the disciples in the synoptic tradition: "You know that those who are supposed to rule over the Gentiles lord it over them, and their great men exercise authority over them. But it shall not be so among you; but whoever would be great among you must be your servant, and whoever would be first among you must be slave of all. For the Son of Man also came not to be served but to serve, and to give his life as a ransom for many" (Mark 10. 42–45; see also Matt. 20. 25–28; Luke 22. 25–27). According to this saying, there can be no analogy with any form of rule or power in the world. On the contrary, it points to the life, mission and service of the Son of Man, Jesus Christ, as the true form of life in the Church.

Consequently, then, in the discussion that follows, the words "democracy", "democratic" and "democratization", when used in the context of the Church, do not have to do with a form of rule or power so much as with a *form of life*. The possible passing on of the basic New Testament law of a Church form of life with the conditions of contemporary society to a democratic form of life in the Church must therefore be directed towards democracy not as a form of rule or power, but as a form of life.[4] Precisely as a sociological and political "thesis of democracy as a form of life of society" as a possible "principle according to which the Church is able to take its place again in contemporary society",[5] the New Testament can name, on the basis of its basic law, the specific conditions of a democratic form of life in the

---

[3] H. Hoefnagels, *Kirche in veränderter Welt* (Essen, 1964), p. 104.
[4] L. Roos, *Demokratie als Lebensform* (Abhandlungen zur Sozialethik 1) (Munich, 1969).   [5] L. Roos, *op. cit.*, p. 346.

Church which will have to reveal the Church in the modern world as a "sign of contradiction". Admittedly, the Church would have first to contradict her present unadapted and levelled down form of life in a fundamental reform. I now propose to outline the New Testament foundations of a democratic form of life in the Church in a short analysis of the basic New Testament law concerning the Church's form of life.

I. Article: The Freedom of Christians

"The Gospel, together with the faith of Christians and the Church as the community of all believers are, according to the New Testament, not factors which prevent, minimalize or suppress freedom—they are, on the contrary, from the theological point of view effective guarantees of freedom, even its ultimate safeguard and foundation. If the Gospel and faith were to disappear from society, freedom would be fundamentally endangered."[6] The "law of freedom" referred to in James 1. 25 and 2. 12 is the law to which Christians have succeeded, because they have accepted faith in the freedom "to which Christ has set them free" (Gal. 5. 1). As the Apostle Paul saw and said so clearly, if the Christian loses the freedom given to him by Christ in God, he will also lose his faith—and therefore also his status as a Christian. If he sacrifices his freedom to any of the powers that may enslave him—and these may be powers in the Church (see Gal. 2)—he will also sacrifice the Gospel and his salvation.

The New Testament concept of freedom,[7] which proclaims that the Christian is not at the disposal of all the powers of this world, should be thought of not in a purely individual sense, but in a social and ecclesiological context. The Christian community, the Church, is above all the fellowship within which eschatological freedom is realized here and now in anticipation, the free fellowship of those who are no longer enslaved and subjected to the elements, the gods, of this world, to the powers of fate or

---

[6] J. Blank, *op. cit.,* p. 35.
[7] See J. Cambier, *La liberté chrétienne selon Saint Paul,* Studia Evangelica II (Berlin, 1964), pp. 315-53; K. Niederwimmer, *Der Begriff der Freiheit im Neuen Testament* (Berlin, 1966); E. Käsemann, *Der Ruf der Freiheit* (Tübingen, 1968).

to the law and the letter of the law, but who have been set free by Christ and are bound only to the "law of Christ" (Gal. 6. 2), to love.

The Christian's freedom is not his dowry as a creature, but the gift of God in the Spirit of Jesus: "Now the Lord is the Spirit, and where the Spirit of the Lord is, there is freedom" (2 Cor. 3. 17). This Pauline affirmation could be readily applied as a norm to the life of the Church. As a gift of God, the Christian's freedom is not at man's disposal, cannot be manipulated and cannot be done away with, if Christianity itself is not to be done away with. The immediate experience of God enjoyed by the Christian, who knows that God has accepted him as a son and has allowed him to call him by the intimate form of address "Abba" (Rom. 8. 14–16), cannot be subjected to further mediation, "for there is one God, and there is one mediator between God and men, the man Jesus, who gave himself as a ransom for all" (1 Tim. 2. 5).

The Christian community, the Church, has, of course, to testify to the truth of the freedom that has been given to her and she can only do this in her form of life. According to the New Testament, this bears the imprint of the free word, frankness, and is characterized by free renunciation, generosity and concern, by the encouragement of lively spontaneity and the banishment of paralysing, legalistic thinking, by liberation from selfishness, from the enslavement of "vital interests" and from fear, by granting peace and joy (Rom. 14. 7), by the destruction of all cramping conventions and by the stimulus of a new unanimity.

The New Testament interprets the Christian's freedom quite radically as freedom from sin and death (Rom. 8. 2) and defines the Christian community consistently as the sphere of life: "We know that we have passed from death to life, because we love the brethren" (1 John 3. 14). The Christian form of life is characterized by *life*, because it is sustained by the "new life of the Spirit" (Rom. 7. 6). The Christian himself is characterized, not by a weak immaturity, but by the practice of freedom, which reminds other people of their freedom, enables them to put it into practice and educates them in its use. The Christian has shining examples for the Christian form of life that is so distinguished by freedom in the activity of Jesus and of Paul.

II. Article: The Equality of Christian Brothers

Christians are "children of the free woman" (Gal. 4. 31) and as such form the community of the free who have been set free for freedom (Gal. 5. 1) and of those who experience God immediately. This fact is expressed in the fundamental equality of Christian brothers. In the Christian community, all the natural and social distinctions which are valid in the world lose their validity and become relative: "For in Christ Jesus you are all sons of God, through faith. For as many of you as were baptized into Christ have put on Christ (like a garment). There is neither Jew nor Greek (distinction between races and religions), there is neither slave nor free (distinction between social classes), there is neither male nor female (distinction between sexes), for you are all one in Christ Jesus" (Gal. 3. 26–29). In the Christian community, every member is equal to every other member, like a brother "for whom Christ died" (Rom. 14. 15) and no member should despise another member or set himself up as a judge over him: "Why do you pass judgment on your brother? Or you, why do you despise your brother? For we shall all (equally) stand before the judgment seat of God" (Rom. 14. 10).

Again, in the Christian community, as before God, there is no discrimination between people: "For if a man with gold rings and in fine clothing comes into your assembly, and a poor man in shabby clothing also comes in, and you pay attention to the one who wears fine clothing and say, 'Have a seat here, please,' while you say to the poor man, 'Stand there,' or 'Sit at my feet,' have you not made distinctions among yourselves, and become judges with evil thoughts?" (James 2. 2–4). The fundamental equality of Christian brothers is based on their freedom and is the prerequisite for the division of the community into many different services (1 Cor. 12). This division of the community or body does not imply any distinction according to class or rank: "God has so adjusted the body, giving the greater honour to the inferior part, that there may be no discord in the body, but that the members may have the same care for one another" (v. 24 f.). No brother may be so presumptuous as to assume a special dignity: "You are not to be called rabbi (master), for you have one teacher (master), and you are all brethren" (Matt. 23. 8).

III. ARTICLE: CHRISTIAN FRATERNITY[8]

The context from which the above quotation (Matt. 23. 8) is taken is one in which the evangelist Matthew, a strong advocate of Christian fraternity, emphasizes Jesus' instructions to his disciples and opposes any kind of "personality cult on the part of Christians which might harm the equality of the brothers".[9] Immediately after the passage quoted above, we read: "And call no man your father on earth, for you have one Father, who is in heaven" (Matt. 23. 9). Within the Christian community, in which all brothers are free and equal, there is no place for any kind of paternalism which might lead to the attempt to establish positions of power and to foster an attitude of immature dependence on the one hand and an attitude of paternal authority, disguised as "spiritual" or "clerical" authority, on the other.[10]

Another passage, Mark 10. 29 ff., expresses almost unintentionally and simply as a matter of fact an ancient tradition that the communities of Jesus have no "fathers". According to this passage, "fathers" form part of everything and everybody left behind by the man who joins the Christian community: "Truly, I say to you, there is no one who has left house or brothers or sisters or mother or father or children or lands, for my sake and for the gospel, who will not receive a hundredfold now in this time, houses and brothers and sisters and mothers and children and lands." This thought can be narrowed down and expressed thus. The patriarch has no place in the community of Jesus. What is of vital importance is the will and kingdom of God and the "form" of this rule of God in Jesus is made manifest and visible as fraternity, brotherly love and an attitude of service to others. The authority which is recognized as valid in the community of the Church is the authority of brotherly love and care. In this fraternity, there can be no authoritarian clerical "father".

Like freedom and equality, Christian fraternity is also a gift (the result of being "children of God") and at the same time a demand. The truth of this fraternity has to be proved in the

---

[8] See J. Ratzinger, *Die christliche Brüderlichkeit* (Munich, 1960).

[9] W. Trilling, "Amt und Amtsverständnis bei Matthäus", in *Mélanges biblique en hommage à B. Rigaux* (Gembloux, 1970), p. 39.

[10] See R. Pesch, "Vater Bischof?", in *Die Bibel kritisch lesen* (Theologia publica, 14) (Olten, 1970), pp. 23-9.

community itself—in mutual admonition and correction and in an unselfish readiness to settle disputes by arbitration. The very name "brother" binds the Christian (see Philem. 16; 1 Cor. 6. 1–11), each to his own special service and task.

IV. Article: The Service of the Christian Community

We possess only very fragmentary information in the New Testament concerning life and order in the early Christian communities, but one of these "gaps" in our information is in fact of the greatest importance. The authors of the New Testament did not use any of the terms which correspond to the modern concept of "office" to denote functions within the Church community and they were surprisingly consistent in their avoidance of these Greek words when they were speaking of services and functions, order and leadership in the Christian community. Whenever they wanted to describe the "services" performed by individuals in the community or to characterize the tasks carried out within the community as a whole or in its missionary activity, they always used a word that "had no association with any special dignity or position",[11] the word *diakonia*. The choice of this word shows clearly that the early Christian authors wanted above all to express a distinctive attitude which prevailed in their communities. This attitude resulted from the freedom, equality and fraternity of Christians who were ready to make themselves available for the task of building up their community. It was above all not an "official" attitude which was based on privilege and authority and from which the obligation to serve arose.

The relevant instructions given to the Christian communities in the synoptic gospels trace this fundamental structure of "office" in the New Testament community back to Jesus himself. One basic statement, for example, is repeated no less than six times with variations: "He who is greatest among you shall be your servant" (Matt. 23. 11, etc.). It is well worth while to get to know, by a few examples, some of the different ways in which this fundamental prophetic norm, by which the evangelists

[11] E. Schweizer, *Gemeinde und Gemeindeordnung im Neuen Testament* (Zürich, 1962), p. 157.

measured the Christian communities and their understanding of the nature of office at different times and places, is expressed in the New Testament. I have already mentioned Jesus' reply to the ten, who had taken offence at the request made by the sons of Zebedee to enjoy the special privilege of exercising power at Jesus' right and left hands (Mark 10. 42–45). I have also drawn attention to the practical consequences for Christian equality and fraternity discussed by Matthew in Chapter 23 of his gospel.

The third evangelist, Luke, gave special emphasis to Jesus' prophetic norm for the New Testament "office" by situating his variation of the theme of the servant in the context of the Last Supper and making the word "servant" the key-word for the function of the apostles. These should, he stresses, be those who serve in the community: "The kings of the Gentiles exercise lordship over them; and those in authority over them are called benefactors. But not so with you; rather let the greatest among you become as the youngest, and the leader as one who serves. For which is the greater, one who sits at table, or one who serves? Is it not the one who sits at table? But I am among you as one who serves" (Luke 22. 25–27).

Finally, in the fourth gospel, the attitude of service that should characterize the Christian in office in the Church is expressed in the symbolic action of the washing of the disciples' feet. This incident, in John 13, occupies the place that is taken up in the synoptic gospels by the accounts of the institution of the Eucharist: "I have given you an example, that you also should do as I have done to you" (John 13. 15).

In all these traditions, then, the mission, life and service of Jesus are shown as examples for the task of the Christian Church. The community of Jesus does not therefore have a power structure such as the one that is present in the world, with its contrasts between rulers or masters and servants, princes and slaves, the first and the last. Under the demands made by the rule and kingdom of God in the mission of Jesus, there is, on the contrary, a complete reversal of these secular norms for those believers who are prepared to change and to build up the community of Jesus. The life and order of the Church community is, according to the basic New Testament law, above all "diaconal", a life and order of service, and a better way of expressing the "democratic" form of life in the Church that is so necessary today would be perhaps a "diaconally democratic" form of life.

V. The Historical Norm of "Office" in the Church

Each of the New Testament communities ordered its life and work and evolved its laws differently, of course, depending on the historical situation and the environment in which it was placed, but generally speaking it did this freely and more or less convincingly as a *diakonia* or service in accordance with the prophetic norm of its "office" provided by Jesus himself. There is documentary evidence to show that this basic New Testament law of *diakonia* was in fact carried out and given a concrete form in various orders of service in the Christian communities. Jesus' prophetic norm is therefore shown in the New Testament to be a historical norm and one which can and indeed must be given a concrete historical form in the life of the Christian Church. A few examples of these "services" in the New Testament will help to make this clear.

As far as can be seen, the different Christian missionary communities, which were founded by Paul in his full power as an apostle and which were, in complete freedom, answerable to him as the servant of the Gospel, were themselves responsible for instituting the various services, orders and functions, the "offices", that were necessary to life in the individual community. There was a group of office-bearers, the leaders, whose task was to serve the community in Thessalonica. They were to be "esteemed very highly because of their work". In other words, their service to the community in the concrete, not their "office" in the abstract, was to make them respected by the community, which furthermore had as much responsibility as the few who had been appointed by the whole community to carry out special tasks (1 Thess. 5. 12 ff.).

In the community at Philippi, there were leaders and preachers who were either elected or else simply confirmed in their "office" by the members of the community and called by secular titles taken from the Greek world of unions and associations—*episkopoi* or overseers and *diakonoi* or servants. This was clearly a step towards the institutionalization of the services or "offices".

I Cor. 16. 15 ff. can be quoted as evidence of the fact that appointment to various necessary services in the communities founded by Paul cannot be regarded as an apostolic ordination on the one hand or as the result of spontaneous enthusiasm on the other. In this passage, we read that Stephanas and his family, who were the first converts in Achaia, placed *themselves* at the service of the community. Paul himself believed that this kind of voluntary service deserved to be recognized as authoritative and that the Christians at Corinth ought to be subject to all those who worked for the community.

This principle can be summarized and expressed thus: *service performed in order to build up the Christian community is always official service.* Every Christian was bound to serve the community according to his abilities and his gifts and there was, at this period, no "office", to which a man had to be appointed or ordained and which was the prerequisite of service to the community. Paul recognized a multiplicity of functions, charisms and so on possessed by individual members of the Christian community (see I Cor. 12. 28; Rom. 12. 4 ff.). They all, he was convinced, had to use their gifts to further the welfare, the unanimity and the peace of the community and they all had to perform an external service, that of building up the community of Christ and of considering those outside the community (I Cor. 14), and an internal service, that of love (I Cor. 13), which is a "still more excellent way" for all.

These New Testament services are above all *collegial offices.* There are many scriptural examples of such collegial offices—the Twelve in the primitive Christian community, the leaders in the Pauline missionary communities and the bishops and elders in the communities of the pastoral letters. These bishops and elders mentioned in these later letters written at the turn of the first Christian century were, as candidates appointed to a clearly defined, already established office by the imposition of hands and were supported in their office by their communities. In addition to the communities referred to in the pastoral letters, which represent an "advanced stage of institutionalization and consolidation",[12] other communities with distinctively fraternal orders of

[12] N. Brox, *Die Pastoralebriefe* (Regensburger Neues Testament, 7, 2) (Regensburg, 1969), p. 42.

service are also mentioned in the later writings of the New Testament (Matthew and John, for example). Towards the end of the period covered by the New Testament, life in the Christian communities and their offices and services were clearly pluriform.

It is not possible to find any evidence in the New Testament for recognizing only one development as authentic. On the contrary, the New Testament can only encourage us to make the decisions confronting the Christian communities today in their search for new forms of life in freedom and responsibility, with full conviction and in accordance with the demands of the present century. In this, we need above all only to be bound by the prophetic norm provided by Jesus himself. This prophetic norm will, as the pastoral letters with their lists of virtues which those in office should possess show us, reveal its sober reality as soon as this is no longer concealed by initial enthusiasm.

VI. Authority in the Church

Service in the Church has to be recognized as authoritative and this authority has already been characterized as an authority of brotherly love and care. Service and authority are in no way mutually exclusive. Both Jesus himself and Paul provide striking examples of the coincidence of service and authority, of the exercise, in service, of truly great authority, that of freedom. "Jesus was, or became, authoritative by what he said and did and this is because his words and actions were felt by men to be helpful, liberating, good and beneficial. In other words, Jesus' authority can be defined as a *full saving power*."[13] Jesus did not resort constantly to this full saving power, nor did he try to justify it or least of all boast of it in an authoritarian manner. On the contrary, he looked for and tried to provoke human freedom. His methods were those of convincing clarity and insight, rational argument and non-casuistical openness and directness. He had authority because all that he said and did arose from the authority of freedom and love and he gave men the power to create, to love and to be free.

No one would accuse Paul of having had an underdeveloped consciousness of his apostolic mission and it is clear that, as the

[13] J. Blank, *op. cit.*, pp. 67 f.

founder of several Christian communities, he claimed the right and the authority to guide and instruct the members of those communities. It really seemed to him "that God has exhibited us apostles as last of all, like men sentenced to death" (1 Cor. 4. 9). He did not regard the authority of his apostolic service as coercive. He asked and directed, admonished and implored and those who listened to him were aware of his authority because it was exercised by a man who had been called freely by grace and was using every rational effort to move others who had also been freely called by grace. "The apostle's authority had an engaging and compelling character because, when he exhorted, he did so as a brother and because he too, like his community, was subject to the same demand"[14]—that of the Gospel and its authority. Paul exercised his special power to lead his communities to freedom and independence, not to keep them in a state of subordination and dependence. "For all things are yours, whether Paul or Apollos or Cephas... all are yours; and you are Christ's; and Christ is God's" (1 Cor. 3. 21 ff.).

CONCLUSION

In sociological and political analyses of democracy as a form of life in society in general, such words are used as fraternity, partnership, solidarity, service, renunciation, trust, freedom, dialogue, tolerance, the common good, willingness to compromise and openness. On the other hand, however, both following and at the same time contradicting this "secular" model, the basic New Testament law of life in the Church can and must be expressed in a contemporary and democratic form of life in the Christian community. This form of life must also be able to make the "additional" freedom, equality and fraternity given to us by God in Jesus Christ visible in the Church, not only as a "sign of contradiction", but also as the "city set on a hill" (Matt. 5. 14) or as the "lamp on a stand" (v. 15 f.) which gives light to the world and is above all *attractive*.

[14] A. Grabner-Haider, *Paraklese und Eschatologie bei Paulus* (Neutestamentliche Abhandlungen, NF 4 (Münster, 1968), p. 46.

Translated by David Bourke

Karl Lehmann

On the Dogmatic Justification for a Process of Democratization in the Church

THE demand for democratization is usually rejected on theological grounds by appealing to certain basic dogmatic and juridical forms belonging to the Church. In contrast with this, the systematic approach adopted in this article is designed to inquire in *positive* terms into the possibilities and limitations of such a demand. Since other articles in this number treat of particular questions in the concrete, it is permissible in this one to confine ourselves to an inquiry into the principles involved.

I. A JUSTIFICATION FOR INCLUDING THE TERM "DEMOCRATIZATION" IN THE LINGUISTIC USAGE OF THEOLOGY

In the demand for democratization a certain *political* concept of democracy is implied, and not infrequently, in applying this term in a theological context, the special problems which it involves are overlooked, or alternatively it is simply taken for granted that in the context involved the term must acquire a special and distinctive stamp. For a discussion of this question in terms of political theory reference may be made to the article by H. Schneider in the present number.[1] At the same time certain points are, nevertheless, indispensable by way of introduction to our present consideration also.

[1] In addition to the bibliography supplied here cf. especially J. Ratzinger and H. Maier, *Demokratie in der Kirche* (Werdende Welt 16) (Limburg, 1970); I. Fetscher, *Die Demokratie* (Stuttgart, 1970) with bibliography.

1. The Formal Interpretation of Democracy

There is no doubt that, taken by itself, a *formal* interpretation of democracy is insufficient in that in itself it includes *only* the principles of citizenship and organization in a state or the written constitution pertaining to it. Nevertheless those who indulge in too hasty a criticism overlook the truth that in this emphasis on the formal elements one vital factor is being pointed to. The "ethical" basis of democracy (e.g., freedom, equality, constitutionality, the principles of government by majority) must not be surrendered for the sake of any particular material gain. In an age which is irrevocably committed to a plurality of ideologies this formal ethos provides an undeniable safeguard against totalitarian claims whether open or concealed.[2]

Yet a concept of democracy which is in principle neutral with regard to value, and radically devoid of material content, is, even in the most favourable circumstances, applicable only to a form of political life between individuals who are completely disunited among themselves or who, at most, are united by the aim of common survival and the impulse to maintain themselves.[3]

To put the matter another way, democracy presupposes in every instance a certain "irreducible minimum of content" for this formal ethos, and it is for the sake of this that a common order of political life is adopted and upon this that unity is arrived at in the form of a certain basic agreement between all those involved. Democracy, therefore, is not merely a system or technique for forming the political will (e.g., election by the people). Rather a special basic value is to be found in the actual principles, e.g., of democratic freedom and political equality, which calls upon the members of this community to defend it—for instance, against aggressors. When we consider the individual *historical* forms in

[2] This is conceded even by critics of a formal interpretation of democracy, e.g., W. Strzelwiéz, "Bürokratisierung der modernen Gesellschaft und die Ohnmacht der Bürgers" in *Hindernisse der Demokratie. Vorträge und Bibelarbeit in der Arbeitsgruppe Demokratie des 14. Deutschen Evangelischen Kirchentags* (Stuttgart, 1969), pp. 19–26, esp. p. 20: "Anyone who condemns the security provided by constitutionality as a mere trivial formality, and is prepared, for the sake of a democratization of the whole of society to destroy it, is acting in just as nonsensical and short-sighted a way as those who acclaim democracy in the constitutional sense without any democratization of the society as a whole."

[3] Cf., e.g., Th. Geiger, *Demokratie ohne Dogma* (Munich, ²1964).

which democracy has been realized, then it becomes apparent that the scope for development, e.g., of freedom and equality (in fact there is a certain tension between those two factors in themselves!) has been relatively variable in the forms which it has assumed at different periods in history.

Admittedly here the borderline between an attitude of participation on the part of the individual in the basic values of democracy which is positive and ever-increasing on the one hand, and the problematic introduction of particular ideas of value into any such concept of democracy on the other, is extremely thin. Here all we can do is to pose this question while leaving it unexplained.[4]

What constitutes the "crux" of all democracy is in fact established by the communication of the optimal amount of freedom and the highest possible degree of equality as two mutually intercommunicating entities. The question of how far these can be achieved cannot altogether be separated from the further question of the possibilities of development open to the individual, and how far these possibilities can *de facto* be realized or what obstacles stand in his path. In other words the question of freedom and equality in their most ideal form cannot be separated from the effective opportunities for development in economic and educational terms that are *de facto* open to all. In any case the politics of a democratic society would incur the danger of being nothing more than the technical administration of an existing social situation, without the possibility of altering for the better the human relationships between individuals. Constitutional democracy *without* any "process of democratization", therefore, constitutes, in the political world as it exists in the concrete, an all but insoluble problem.

2. On the Problems entailed in the Material Concept of Democracy

But this is the precise point of entry at which a certain material interpretation of democracy inserts itself, often quite unreflectingly: democracy then appears as the dynamic process by which an *integral* equality of opportunity is brought to its fullness in the political, economic and social areas of human living. On this showing democracy becomes a factor which transforms the

[4] For more precise details on this, cf. M. Hättich, *Demokratie als Herrschaftsordnung* (Ordo Politicus 7) (Cologne, 1967), with bibliography.

constitution of *all* spheres of human living, re-orientating them to this end. Certain aspects of this concept of democracy belong in principle to the history of the movement of emancipation which is proper to the new age.[5] But it acquires, at least in *one* respect, a quite fundamental predetermination. For it is *presupposed* that the process thus conceived of, of transforming the constitution of society, represents the essential content of democracy both in its questions any further at this point.[6]

Even if we were to fall in with any decision with regard to the "basic facts" involved in such an assumption, still this would only be indirectly to forestall the further question of *how* this comprehensive transformation is to be achieved. By what right is this concept of democracy *a priori* extended so as to cover the whole of society in all its aspects? Can we bring *all* the special factors in a society (e.g., including its economy, its society, schools, armed forces, administration, churches, families) under a single organizational principle? We shall not be pursuing these questions any further at this point.[6]

A still more important point is the following: in any *conception* of democracy which is predetermined beforehand in this way one factor is already anticipated, and the consensus which needs to be obtained upon it is already presupposed. This is that toilsome process of forming the common will in the concrete in a society which still needs to be achieved. And this is forestalled and presupposed, even though it still has to be sought out and established, and even though the only way of doing this is through a rational and democratic process of arriving at the decision of the majority. The *"volonté générale"* is already determined *beforehand* in respect of its *content*. Now the dangers involved in such an understanding of democracy are quite palpable. When a (homogeneous) regulation is imposed on all areas of social life *equally*, then it is quite impossible to prevent "totalitarian"[7]

[5] Admittedly this does not imply that other aspects, e.g., the principle of representation, are merely an expression of the decay and distortion of an original concept of democracy. Cf. also on this, I. Fetscher, *op. cit.*

[6] On this cf. the controversial study by W. Hennis, *Demokratisierung. Zur Problematik eines Begriffs* (Cologne, 1970). With this work at least we must take issue.

[7] On the phenomenon of totalitarianism, cf. W. Schlangen, "Der Totalitarismus-Begriff", in *Aus Politik und Zeitgeschichte*, Supplement to the weekly journal, *Das Parlament* 44 (31 Oct. 1970).

tendencies. At the same time there is the threat of imposing a radical political stamp[8] upon all spheres of life and upon human awareness in general. The state and the society both move towards a mutual identification at least as a matter of tendency.

From this it is clear that any *unconsidered adoption* of a material understanding of democracy entails dangers which are not inconsiderable. At the same time a further point which is made apparent in this connection is the *formal* dimension of constitutional democracy in all its indispensable necessity. The theologian who speaks of "democratization of (or in) the Church" must be aware of *what* particular concept of democracy he is implicitly using. In assuring himself of this the theologian will not merely be contributing to the clarity of his own ideas, but will also be fulfilling a responsibility which is indispensable in theology, and one which he incurs when he enters, at least indirectly, upon "secular" spheres, and in this case political ones, and encounters predetermined judgments whether implicit or explicit (and possibly politically effective ones) on this question of democracy.

He can all too easily fall into the "naïveté" of demanding movements which run counter to democracy in the true sense. Not infrequently the theologian is too careless in his approach to certain structures of common human living which are sharply differentiated from one another and extremely vulnerable, which have been painfully worked out and can only retain their distinctive forms so long as a delicate balance between them is maintained. Now these structures are suddenly torn out of their context by the theologian, and their very existence is endangered. The theologian's responsibility to the world prohibits him, in such contexts, from any oversimplification or even deficiencies in his awareness of the problems involved.[9]

---

[8] This must be distinguished from the consciousness of the political importance of these areas, as also of the importance of awakening or maintaining in wakefulness an attitude of readiness to take responsibility in political life.

[9] This demand derives primarily from a scientific postulate because it has to do with the implications of a theory which has been put forward. The political decisions of the theologian in the concrete (e.g., for a particular party) must be set apart from this.

3. Anthropological and Ethical Substructures of Democracy in the Concrete

A further point, admittedly, which has also become evident, is that the simple distinction between "formal" and "material" is inadequate, however indispensable it may still remain in any attempt at sketching in the basic outlines of the problem. Democracy as a political order in the *concrete* is certainly connected with other factors apart from purely formal principles. But as a pattern of political organization it is also not the sole form of human living or the absolute good[10] for *all* departments of human existence. This point is certainly compatible with the conviction that democracy is the only form of social and constitutional organization which is acceptable today.

The rational process of arriving at a common basic interest must in fact have been discovered in working out from day to day the processes of common human living. It is necessary for those involved to respect one another as partners and to have become accustomed to this as a firmly rooted attitude. It is also necessary for them to have acquired a firm awareness of their responsibilities and a state of mind in which priority is accorded to rational argument. Without these necessary factors democracy cannot, in the long run, survive as a constitutional form of life. In this sense "democracy" is sustained by the associations, groups and institutions involved submitting themselves to a freely elected organization, disciplining themselves and taking responsible decisions on the various aspects of their common life. For democracy to be brought to its true fullness, therefore, as a constitutional *reality*, it is surely necessary to invoke something in the nature of specific anthropological, social and ethical conditions which are necessary for its efficient functioning.

By means of this concept of democracy as a "form of life"[11]

[10] Admittedly such a statement is open to contradiction. Better: its validity depends on the particular interpretation of democracy presupposed in any given case. We may compare, for example, the definition of Th. Wilhelm (ed.), *Demokratie in der Schule* (Paedagogica 7) (Göttingen, 1970), pp. 8 f.: "Democracy is here taken to mean that experiment which needs constantly to be revised, to create those social conditions which permit the life of the individual citizen to be as free as possible from authority, while avoiding all élitist or egalitarian ideologies." On this cf. below, Section VI.

[11] On this cf. C. J. Friedrich, *Demokratie als Herrschafts- und*

and a "style" we can convey the difference between the formal
and material understanding of democracy in positive terms,
though admittedly, in adopting this approach, we do not *ipso
facto* demand a simultaneous and harmonious transformation of all departments of life, which *de facto* threatens
to become identified with a radical invasion of political
organization into them all. In this sense democracy considered as a political reality is connected with certain prior
conditions of an anthropological and ethical nature (e.g.,
respect for human dignity, solidarity, partnership, freedom, etc.).
Now the precise content of the convictions of basic value which
have been brought into harmony and are held in common appears
to be, *within certain limits*, a variable factor (cf. III, 1). And because of this any given interpretation of democracy which is
made real and binding at a particular epoch is, from the point of
view of basic politics, only binding in this sense for the time
being. On the other hand (if we abstract from certain specific
elements), it is hardly possible to arrive at any suprahistorical or
universal concept of democracy. In any case such a concept has
very little value considered as a general "blueprint" with a universal application.

II. Analogies to Democracy as the Basic Elements in the Christian "Form of Life"

In any application of the concept of democracy to the ecclesiastical entity we must take these basic problems into consideration. Any merely formalistic principle of democracy would only
serve to introduce certain isolated political techniques and
methods of procedure, although admittedly, provided certain
conditions are met, there is nothing to be objected to in these.
If we were to adopt a material concept of democracy (in principle in the sense discussed above) then this would, if carried
through to its logical conclusions, have the effect of classifying the
Church more or less without distinction among all other spheres
of social living.

Lebensform (Heidelberg, 1959), and especially L. Roos, *Demokratie als
Lebensform* (Abhandlungen zur Sozialethik 1) (Munich, 1969), especially,
pp. 292 ff.

Moreover, by altering the distinctive conditions which are proper to her own nature it would have the effect of "bringing her into line with" the general process of constitutional transformation. To the extent that the Church lives in the context of the modern and democratic world, the greatest possible "democratization" of her organization is admittedly necessary, though this certainly does not mean that from the theological point of view[12] she must undergo any fundamental change of structure or any radical loss of identity. It is in this that the "problem" of the democratization of "the" Church, or alternatively *in* the Church, consists.

1. *"Communio" and "Brotherhood" as Substructures*

Here too we should take as our starting-point the idea of democracy as a "form of life" in the sense defined above, and, on the basis of this presentation of the question, seek for analogies, above all for the anthropological and ethical presuppositions to it. In fact the correspondence we are seeking for here can be attained to methodologically on historical and systematic grounds. The initial impulse which led to the development of certain elements in democracy was provided by the Christian stock of ideas, however mistaken the attitude of individual Christians may have been in history to these "runaway children" of Christianity itself. In effect the very fact that the Christian Churches represent a union of members who have come together of their own free decision is in itself sufficient to constitute an intrinsic approximation to democracy.

The very fact that the radically free and personal act of faith by which membership of the Church is primarily constituted (for

---

[12] Cf. the study by J. Ratzinger, *op. cit* (n. 1); K. Rahner, "Demokratie in der Kirche?", *Gnade als Freiheit* (Freiburg, 1968), pp. 113–30; *idem, Freiheit und Manipulation in Gesellschaft und Kirche* (Münchener Akademie-Schriften 53) (Munich, 1970); O. Semmelroth, R. Haubst, K. Rahner, eds., *Martyria—Leiturgia—Diakonia. Festschrift für H. Volk* (Mainz, 1968), pp. 399–415; J. G. Gerhartz, "Demokratisierung in der Kirche", *Theologische Akademie* 6 (Frankfurt, 1969), pp. 88–115; M. Kaiser, "Kann die Kirche demokratisiert werden?" *Lebendiges Zeugnis* (1969), pp. 5–21; H. Hoefnagels, *Demokratisierung der kirchlichen Autorität* (Vienna, 1969); A. Müller, *Kirchenreform heute* (Munich, 1968); cf. also *Demokratisierung der Kirche in der Bundesrepublik Deutschland. Ein Memorandum deutscher Katholiken*, ed. by the Bensberger Circle (Mainz, 1970).

the moment we are abstracting from the question of infant baptism) means that there are certain sustaining elements in the basic nature of the Church which exhibit points of contact with the ethos of democracy as a form of life. The freedom of the children of God, the universal priesthood, the imparting of the Spirit to all (charismata), the conscious holding of faith in common on the part of the believers, the basic equality of Christians, the equality of dignity attached to the name of Christian and other elements provide a basis for this fundamental structure (for details cf. R. Pesch's article written for this number). Additional strength is imparted to this factor by the fundamental reality that all are there for one another and with one another, working from the life-principle of brotherhood and brotherly love. The specific concepts of community (*koinonia, communio*), of collegiality and of solidarity are only the outward forms of this fundamental characteristic of the Church.

2. *The Christian Ethos and Democratic Structures*

In connection with this it is certain, first of all, that a basic spiritual demand is expressed in Holy Scripture: solicitude for one another in an intense degree, a radical concern for the interests of one's neighbour, a surrender of one's personal life on behalf of one's brother, an understanding for those who are differently constituted, mutual forgiveness, "vicariousness" (taking another's life upon one's self), etc. On no account must this be reduced to a mere "spiritualizing".

But it is also undeniable that this fundamental reality, this demand which is made upon Christian living in Scripture and in the early Church still does not, in itself, represent a directly *juridical and institutional* basic constitution. It is the form of life lived in the existing circumstances in the concrete, and also the effective basis for it, and these two factors taken together determine all human relationships in the concrete in the community. Now "prior to" all juridically and institutionally assured procedures the intrinsic depths of an invisible substructure of this kind to the Christian life as lived in the concrete implies a fundamental ethos, Nowhere are freedom, partnership, brotherhood and mutual service, considered as the necessary prior conditions for any co-existence of this kind, more plainly evident than in a

Church brought together by God's sovereign grace into a "communion of saints". The common state of being-in-Christ ("*Christus totus*") is the basis in life for this "democratic" existence.

It is true that this does not provide any institutionalized pattern for the common life of the Church. But at the same time we must in principle guard against relegating these structures exclusively to the realm of an unworldly "mental attitude". There is no need to do this either from considerations of a falsely spiritualizing interiorization. Certainly there is a kind of "brotherliness" at the spiritual and pastoral level which actually does the greatest possible harm to this fundamental brotherhood. It is here that we come to the critical point: the sort of "brotherliness" which remains only at the level of a moralizing slogan and appeal, usually applied only to one's neighbour, but which never finds expression in new forms, remains, in the deepest sense, ambiguous.

The Christian community can only succeed as a brotherhood when this goal is also given real embodiment in the systems and social interrelationships in which we live. The spiritual dimensions of Christian brotherliness should not prevent us from entering wholeheartedly into these practical and down-to-earth ways of giving it reality. If the spiritual dimensions do not carry enough spiritual power and real conviction to make their impact and to imprint themselves deeply upon these present forms of human co-existence, then they are indeed unlikely to be effective in any sense. For this reason it must not be made impossible for these basic elements in a Christian community to express themselves in those forms of fulfilment found in the contemporary world which have a stronger element of rationality in them as a result of having been thought out in common.

The interconnection and interplay of "interior" and "exterior" elements can become a real touchstone by which to prove the concrete truth of fine words and "attitudes" which are constantly invoked. For instance there would have been no founding of orders if the charisms had not been able to break out and to transcend the constitutional structures in all their spontaneity and explosive force. If the institutional elements allowing for this had not already been in existence, then they would have had to be created at the time. Why should this not be possible, within certain limits, for other forms of living in the Church as well?

3. *The Opportunities for and the Limits to an Institutionalization of Democracy as a "Way of Life"*

Nevertheless the devising of forms for this does not *ipso facto* or necessarily have to imply a juridical or "political" system. It would be the worst possible pattern which could be devised on the basis of a formalistic understanding of democracy if we were to lay the emphasis exclusively upon the constituent elements, e.g., the assigning of jurisdiction, the division of power, the factor of majority decision, etc. "Brotherhood", for instance, is a more comprehensive *principle* of life. We can attain to a greater possibility of discussion and agreement, for example, by way of *counsel* (so long as we are aware of the effectiveness of really good counsel) than by defining the limits of specific "rights". The personal example of a good official of the government in word and behaviour, for instance, can lead to a "democratization" of the whole style of social, constitutional or even ecclesiastical procedures, which can hardly, if at all, be achieved through legal enactments.

It is not always the institutions, therefore, that need to be perfected. But anyone who reacts against the transformation of many forms which have hitherto existed as powers to instruct into forms of counsel and common resolution, or who seeks only to establish the "spirit", for instance, of brotherliness, almost necessarily loses credibility today. Many forms of authoritative behaviour can and should be abolished. In all hierarchies forms of communication between the "rulers" and "ruled" have been traditionalized. Today these are anachronistic, and therefore in the process of disappearing. Every official representative today must recognize which particular ways of performing his function can be adopted so as to produce a state of corporate participation, partnership and co-operation.

Precisely in those cases where the enticements of power have become common and habitual, and are characterized by modes of behaving which are autocratic, that kind of authority which is genuinely ready to accept reform can commit itself to the obligations of concrete forms of partnership or mutual respect for the views of different parties through institutional "safeguards" and common ways of procedure.

Moreover, those who are ready wholeheartedly to give themselves to the service of others should not be afraid to commit themselves by an unambiguous assent to accepting ways in which others can play a responsible part in the taking of decisions. This is still not to exclude the exercise of a veto in decisions of principle when there are good reasons for this.

The hesitation of many hierarchical authorities (not only in the Church) to agree to such procedures, and their practice of appealing again and again merely to established attitudes in response to all those who demand "democratization" tempts these to regard all exhortations of this kind merely as attempts to inculcate the "spirit" of submissiveness, and to this end all the more resolutely to suppress (even by political means of oppression and with admonitions to obedience) the demands for structural and technical changes to be introduced. These again are misinterpreted by the "opponents" as so many "external" and organizational superficialities. In practice both the upholders of the demand for democratization and the groups who oppose it very often regard it without taking into account the fact that it is rooted in the context of the more basic demands for democracy as a "way of life", and for this reason it not infrequently becomes a barren object of strife between the two opposing fronts. Only when the substructures and sustaining forces of "democracy" are taken into consideration is it possible to arrive at any meaningful plan for democracy. This also applies to the ecclesiastical and theological sphere.

III. On the Existence of Constitutional Elements which cannot be altered

There are various ways of achieving an approximation to the central problem in the relationship of a concept of democracy to ecclesiastical structures. For instance, we may examine various analogies between the two (cf., for example, synodal elements, the charismatic principle, the common awareness of faith held by the people of God as a whole, etc.).[13] Elements from the secular form of democracy as a constitutional reality which are capable of finding a corresponding application in the contemporary Church[14] might also be found, for instance, the strengthening of constitutional principles (above all a greater possibility of establishing what is just, developing means of protecting the rights of the individual),[15] certain aspects of the division of authority (on this cf. P. Huizing's article in this number), the development of constitutional jurisdiction, collaboration in the appointment of officials (on this cf. the article by R. Kottje in this number), the most important committees conducting their business as far as possible in public (on this cf. the article by J. Remy), etc.

Even when these indispensable concrete applications have been achieved (cf. VI below) the factor which is basic to the whole system still remains indeterminate and ambiguous, and when this is treated of it is not infrequently designated as the "sovereignty of the people", something which, in the last analysis, is totally unacceptable so far as the Church is concerned, since here the only dominion which can be in question is that of Jesus Christ. But though this distinction is in itself correct,[16] it does not contribute any greater clarity since even in the conception of democracy proper to the new age and actually entertained since the time of Rousseau the element of *direct* sovereignty of the people has in any case been realized only to a limited extent (on this cf. the article by H. Schneider).[17]

1. *A Consideration of the "Basic Substance" of the Democratic Form of Constitution*

A point which we have already discussed (cf. I, 1) is that every

[13] Cf. in this sense the approach adopted by J. Ratzinger, K. Rahner, O. Semmelroth, J. G. Gerhartz in the studies referred to in n. 12.

[14] Examples in H. Maier, *op. cit.* (n. 1), pp. 69–77.

[15] In many periods of its history prior to 1918 canon law explicitly recognized greater possibilities, e.g., of appeal than today.

[16] On this cf., from the aspect of political philosophy, H. H. Hofmann (ed.), *Die Entstehung des modernen souveränen Staates* (Neue Wissenschaftliche Bibliothek 17) (Cologne, 1967, with bibliography); B. de Jouvenel, *Über Souveränität* (Neuwied, 1962).

[17] In greater detail also in I. Fetscher, *op. cit.* (n. 1), pp. 20 ff.

concept of a basic democratic order presupposes a minimum content of agreement as to the basic aims of a society. This cannot be established simply by some kind of authority. Rather it underlies —at least within certain definite limits which we shall shortly be speaking of—the right of a people to self-determination. The process of forming the political will is, in a certain sense, the decisive factor in determining the basic form of the constitution at any given time. Here an important line of demarcation has undoubtedly to be drawn between the conception of democracy and the idea of the Church. For although in the Church too a certain transformation does take place in faith, dogma and law,[18] still, from this point of view the very nature of the Church (as instituted by Jesus Christ for the salvation of mankind, which they are utterly incapable of providing for themselves) is such that no total right of self-determination exists in her as a society in view of her foundations as a society.

Now there is a further distinction too which must not be overlooked: the conception of democracy of the new age also recognizes limits in the degree to which the basic structure can be altered ("unalterable constitutional law").[19] Certain definite basic principles which go to make up the "basic substance" of the constitution, and thereby the identity of a given community also, are set apart from the political manoeuvres which are carried on from day to day. On these no vote can be taken in the true sense. Without them (e.g., the equality of rights between individuals, the regime being answerable to the voters for its actions, the obligation of the government to observe the law, the independence of the courts, the guaranteeing of freedom and equality of opportunity between the parties, at least in the initial stages of their competition with one another), it is impossible to exclude the element of arbitrariness from the government. Only with them can a form of politics which is acceptable to all be carried on even when

[18] Precisely because of the analogy explained in what follows, the "essential difference" between the political interpretation of democracy and the Church must not be pressed too far. This is something that is demonstrated by H. Maier, op. cit. (in n. 1), pp. 71 ff.

[19] Further on the constitutional effectiveness, e.g., of the Federal Republic of Germany, cf. H. Ehmke, Grenzen der Verfassungsänderung (Tübingen, 1953); K. v. Beyme, Die verfassungsgebende Gewalt des Volkes (Tübingen, 1968).

the minorities who have been defeated at the polls are still living
freely in a united nation of this kind.

2. The Limitations of the Analogy

Admittedly—and in point of fact this constitutes a fundamental
point of difference—the possibility of control over the "basic substance" of the constitutional reality is still narrower in the Church.
Precisely in the concept of self-determination in the full sense,
which is something more than a power to give counsel or a right
to *contribute* to decisions on the part of the governed, a postulate
which has been included in principle ever since the seventeenth
century is that of a *total* dependence of the rulers on the confidence of those who, as the "people", remain the ultimate subject
of the decisions taken. In the Church, on the other hand, the
basic elements—namely the revelation of Jesus Christ as expressed
in the dimension of a truth to be accepted by faith and, arising
from this, the ethical principles and the basic institutional form
of the Church—are, to a large extent, set apart from the area
which the members of the Church have power to control for
themselves.

This does not exclude the fact that God has bestowed upon the
Church a right understanding of the Gospel both as a gift and
as a task which she has to perform in the world maturely and
responsibly, and that this in turn gives her the right to a certain
scope for freedom in order that she may interpret and apply the
basic truth which has thus been bestowed upon her in the sphere
of history. But even here the fact still remains that all the activities
designed to achieve an effective application of the Gospel in concrete history in this sense continue to be primarily and radically
subject to a right hearing of the "word of God". Here a duty of
obedience arises from the very "fact" of revelation, which, in
fact, we need not shrink from subjecting to any kind of rational
examination, but yet at the same time which recognizes no
autonomous power of control over that which has been entrusted
to it.

Christian faith does indeed demand that the recipient of it shall
in every respect act as a partner, free and subject to no compulsion
whatever. But it cannot eliminate from its nature an acknowledged dependence of man upon God. If God is, in Jesus Christ,

the *Kyrios* of the world, then *this particular* "dominion" can never be totally reconstituted in a democratic form.

3. The Wide Scope for Change which Exists in Practice

If we sought to work out in more precise detail what this "basic substance" in the life of the Church which is not subject to our control consists in, we would have to give an account of the "essence of Christianity" in all its fundamental aspects. In doing this we would have to adopt a more cautious approach today with regard to the dogmatic statements of faith and the institutional elements which go to make up the Church as it has evolved in history, in order to establish what really is "unalterable" in Christianity.

Far too much of that which has grown up from quite specific situations and circumstances belonging to particular epochs in the way of views and characteristic forms has been pronounced "unalterable" or "eternal" by theologians and canon lawyers. In any case a precise delimitation cannot be achieved for all areas of the Church's life or on a global scale.

The distinctions can only be worked out in the actual experience of the Church's life in the concrete. This is a task which does not belong to the more limited scope of this article. It is sufficient for our present purposes that the *actual fact* has been made clear in principle *that* there are in the Church expressions of faith and of law which man has indeed been charged with the duty of giving historical form, yet which in fact derive from the task and the testament bequeathed by Christ and as such are not subject to man's control.

IV. The Official Organization of the Church and the Concept of Democracy

In order to apply this basic idea in the concrete brief examples must be given drawn from that area of the Church's life which seems most of all to present obstacles with regard to the demand for a process of democratization, namely the official organization of the Church. Attempts at radical democratization of this official organization of the Church, for instance, by interpreting the universal priesthood of the faithful as a democratic principle which can be applied to the life of the spirit, are not new, even though they are again and again seized upon as a novelty.[20]

1. The Problems entailed in, and the Various Aspects of, the Term "Official" as applied to the Ministry of the Church

It is, after all, significant that the New Testament knows no term for officialdom which ascribes any superiority to the individuals vested with it. On the contrary, all authority (and it is indisputable that there is authority) is characterized with a certain uniformity as being at most "ministry" or "service" (*diakonia*). What this term is intended to cover is first and foremost special tasks and special gifts which are aimed strictly at serving others. Moreover, all those commissioned with such tasks are characterized as "servants (slaves) of Jesus Christ". In view of these facts we may even hesitate to use the term "official" at all.

Even if it is not used in the New Testament in a general sense, still it must be admitted that it can comprise and express certain indispensable elements, especially in the post-Easter commission given by Jesus Christ to his Church, as a term expressing the retrospective reflections of the early Christians (the same applies, for instance, to the term "sacrament"). But although such terms expressing the reflections of the early Church are indispensable, they must also be tested again and again in the manner in which they are used in the concrete to see whether certain tendencies latent in them are becoming too strong and beginning to predominate—tendencies which they carry with them from their independent usage is *secular* contexts (e.g., dominion, self-assertion, power, authority), but which, according to the New Testament, are not admissible in this form in the exercise of the Christian ministry.

Here we come to an inevitable dividing of the ways. The term "ministry" as used in the New Testament sense should not, on this account, mislead us into a purely functional view of the mission that stems from Christ and the task that has to be accomplished through him. It is right that, when an official body has been set up to minister in some particular way on behalf of the

---

[20] Fuller details are provided in a work to which too little attention is paid today, namely O. Linton, *Das Problem der Urkirche in der neueren Forschung* (Uppsala, 1932, reprinted Frankfurt, 1960).

community in the name of Jesus Christ, its actual performance, wholly at the concrete level, should be subject to examination, and that the manner in which such official bodies function should be inquired into. But this task should not lead on to an attack on authority formally as such. Nevertheless the manner in which the ministry of the Church has been divided up has not been haphazard, i.e., dictated by the particular needs which arise from time to time, and therefore merely spasmodic.

Now whatever claims may be put forward by a particular office-holder in particular circumstances, the fact is that this ministry can, in a certain sense, be withdrawn from the individual holder and therefore, without underestimating the importance of the personal element, we can say that it requires a certain permanence and firmness of outline as an institution in its own right. (For instance, the concrete necessities require that the "post" shall once more be filled.) To this extent, therefore, we can speak unreservedly, and with a special kind of historical justification,[21] of ecclesiastical "office".

2. *The Office is, in its "Ultimate Essence", not subject to Human Control*

The distinctive characteristic of this office consists in the fact that in itself it recognizes no *independent* authority. Power in the Church is nothing else than the power of Jesus himself. In the light of the New Testament we can only speak of this "office" in any meaningful way so long as it remains subordinated to the ministry and power of Jesus Christ. It is the authorization of the crucified Lord, which is complemented by a readiness for unreserved service and for the "lowliness" which this "official" activity entails. Of itself alone and in isolation this "office" is nothing.

Its justification and its "unique quality" is to be found only in a radical abandonment of all positions of power and an attitude in which the subject sets himself free for that which this "office"

---

[21] On the ways in which the doctrine and practice of the papacy have influenced the shaping of the concept of the place of officialdom in society cf. W. Ullmann, *Papst und König. Grundlagen des Papstums und der englishchen Verfassung im Mittelalter* (Dike 3) (Salzburg, 1966), pp. 20–22 (with bibliography).

guarantees. It is only because he, the Lord, lives on in the ministry of his servant that there is any "authority" attached to this office. Hence, too, theological tradition tells us that it is Jesus Christ himself who baptizes, preaches and celebrates the Eucharist (cf. the Constitution on the Liturgy, No. 7). It is because Jesus Christ, after his death and resurrection, wills to be present on behalf of mankind in the *world of history*, and that too as his own self, that this mission exists through him, and owes its existence to no other source beside him. It is only in virtue of his will as founder, his will, that is to say, to make all men sharers in the fruits of his life and work—at least by offering them grace and salvation—that we find a real basis for there being any "offices", understanding these in a strictly christological sense, in the Church. Primitive Christianity, therefore, was perfectly right in regarding the official positions in the ecclesiastical community, which were only fully developed in the post-Easter Church, not primarily as mere functional or organizational entities, designed to facilitate the activities of the community, but *primarily* as a gift of the glorified Lord to his Church.

The existence of such official positions, therefore, is due not to any missionary zeal, and still less merely to the need for a division of labour and demarcation of authority in the community. This is made apparent not only in Luke and in the Pastoral Epistles, but also in Paul. Recent exegesis of 2 Corinthians 5. 18–20 shows that the "ministry of reconciliation" as such springs directly from the death of the Lord on behalf of all and from his resurrection.[22] Since, therefore, it is the will of Jesus Christ himself that this ministry shall be a part of his own authority, it follows that whatever human influences may have been brought to bear on the precise form it has assumed, this ministry, as belonging intrinsically to the authority of Jesus Christ himself, did not derive primarily from any human initiative.

3. *Abuses, and yet "Divine Origin"*

In many respects it is certain that traditional theology has been

---

[22] Cf. also only E. Dinkler, "Die Verkündigung als eschatologisch-sakramentaler Geschehen. Auslegung von 2 Kor 5:14–6:2", G. Bornkamm, K. Rahner, *Die Zeit Jesu. Festschrift für H. Schlier* (Freiburg, 1970), pp. 169–89.

too hasty in ascribing certain elements, forms of expression and modes of manifestation in this official ministry to the dimension of its immutable origin, i.e., to "divine right" (*jus divinum*), and thereby has mistakenly pronounced many elements in it inviolate and beyond criticism. The critico-historical approach to exegesis and Church history has shown that although there is a level in these official positions in the Church which is ordained by God as inviolate in this sense, and so not for man to alter, still it needs to be far more narrowly circumscribed. But at the same time it has also become clear through these findings that the *existence* and "nature" of the "official ministry" understood precisely in *this* sense do in fact belong to those "primary factors" which cannot be set aside in any process of "democratizing" the Church.

This does not mean that we are seeking to bar the way to a far-reaching reform, or to those changes in the form of the Church's official ministry which go with this, by imposing limits which could have the effect of acting as apologetic, or even ideological props to support certain cravings for authority. On the contrary, it is only by isolating and defining the irreducible minimum of content which admittedly cannot be removed in the official ministry[23] that scope can be provided, and thereby a surprising degree of freedom assured, in the re-shaping of the Church's official ministry.

It must be conceded that it is only when we view this ministry in its character as being ultimately christological in origin that we can understand that *for this very reason* an inalienable responsibility is to be attributed to it *uniquely*, one which, while it cannot be separated from the community, is not to be seen either as deriving from it alone; one which, in virtue of the will of Jesus Christ as founder of the Church, belongs to the "immutable constitutional rights" of the Church.

It is self-evident that this does not exclude some form of participation by the community, for instance in the appointment of

[23] On this cf. provisionally K. Lehmann, "Das priesterliche Amt im priesterlichen Volk", in *Klerusblatt* 50 (1970), pp. 315–19, which also appears in the collected papers of the Trier Catholic Conference 1970, *Gemeinde des Herrn* (Paderborn, 1970). Cf. also the study referred to in n. 25.

an individual to an office in the Church. How we are to maintain our recognition of this "authority" inherent in the official ministry of the Church and still accord due value to the part to be played by the community as a whole must now be made the subject of a special concluding discussion in its own right.

V. THE FREEDOM OF THE CHRISTIAN AND THE CHURCH'S OFFICIAL AUTHORITY

There is no room in the Church for that kind of authoritarianism which amounts to a demand for an attitude of unconditional submissiveness and an uncritical recognition of the claims of authority or its unrestricted exercise (on this cf. the articles by R. Pesch and N. Greinacher). True authority is that quality which exists in virtue of a fully thought-out *assent* to an offering of guidance or a claim upon the individual's active collaboration, and achieves recognition on this basis.

1. *The Meaning of Official Authority*

In the Church every kind of basic qualification to hold office ultimately derives from the authority of Jesus Christ. Now if this is true, then it follows, with regard to the question of what the basis for this authority is, that it can never *formally as such* be transmitted *wholly* "from below". This is perfectly reconcilable with the principle that every exercise of official authority must remain constantly rooted in the soil of a community conceived of in terms of brotherhood and collegiality.

The fact that "officialdom" and authority in the Church are first and foremost "christocratic" in their basis and structure means that in practice they should never lead to man dominating over man.[24] What they constitute, rather, is nothing else than that which makes present the *one* bringer of salvation, Jesus Christ, and in themselves they are nothing else than the most radical surrender of personal interests in the service of this one

---

[24] On the problems involved in the use of the concept of dominion cf. O. Brunner, "Bemerkungen zu den Begriffen 'Herrschaft' und 'Legitimät' ", in *Neue Wege der Verfassungs- und Sozialgeschichte* (Göttingen, [2]1968), pp. 64–79; for the theological aspects cf. H. Dembowski, *Grundfragen der Christologie, erörtert am Problem der Herrschaft Jesu Christi* (Munich, 1969).

unique "power". Where abuses of official positions and authoritarian attitudes exist, these must be criticized on the basis of their actual performance. But they do not demand any absolute or radical abolition of all such official positions and authority as such.

In the light of the content of faith there is no room for any discrimination between the "rulers" and "ruled", because all together must belong first and foremost to their one Lord. The community will also be thankful when a brother in the faith preaches the Gospel of Jesus Christ to them in that spirit of service and dedication which is appropriate to a minister in the fullest possible sense (i.e., to a "supreme official"), and acts "in Christ's place" (2 Cor. 5. 20) to make actual in the present the reality of his salvation. The "holder of office" himself will be conscious of belonging primarily to the community of the believers. In many respects he must constantly be searching for the word of truth in company with his fellow believers. Nor does he in any sense "possess" salvation—least of all for himself.

All will also be aware, from their own personal Christian lives, of the fact that the message of Jesus Christ is not a reality that is immediately self-evident and which will be accepted by man without contradiction. The necessity for a constant adaptation of ideas and for constant renewal in faith, hope and love makes it clear that the word of exhortation, of demand, of repentance, and the imperative which summons men to transform their lives must apply to *everyone*. So long as such a word, "strange" and sometimes "hard" as it may be on the part of the preacher, is restricted to putting into force what God wills for men and from them, then any "authority" of this kind cannot be interpreted as dominion on the part of *man*.

2. *The Christian Heritage of the Community and Official Authority in it understood as a Trusteeship*

The holder of office must himself develop a "mode of presentation" which conveys to the rest of his fellow believers the fact that in his official activities it is only their own essential "heritage" that he is engaged upon and striving to promote. When the community as a whole realizes and accepts this as their common conviction, seeing it as part of their call to accept the love of Jesus Christ that frees them, and when they give it reality in

their faith, their worship and their brotherly love for one another, then the very meaning of the Christian community is such
as to leave no further room for any playing off of freedom
against authority, the official ministry against the charismatic
elements, official direction against "democratization", "authority" against "guidance by the Spirit".

Authority can exist only because all assent to, and will to extend the dominion of the *Kyrios*. For this reason the community
will not feel that any discordant note has been struck by the
selfless guidance of the official ministers of the Church, a guidance which remains wholly in line with the will of Jesus Christ
as founder. On the contrary (subject to the conditions mentioned
above) they will be able to recognize in this guidance what they
themselves will to achieve. Provided the official minister restricts
himself radically to what is essential to his function, what he is
doing is to undertake a trusteeship which ultimately speaking
every Christian recognizes and assents to. This is that unshake-
able cleaving to the Gospel, to the creed and to the (fundamental)
ethical principles of the Church to which all are bound, and
which represents an unceasing duty to stand fast by the essence
of the Christian message and a certain safeguard against any tendency to despotism on the part of the individual subject.

To a large extent, therefore, "authority" can be viewed in the
context of the community also. Moreover, a point which is clearest
of all in this context is that however necessary it may be sharply
to distinguish between two different entities (e.g., the official
ministry and the community) from certain aspects, still precisely
this tendency to introduce a dichotomy between the two needs
to be tested and examined to see whether we have not overlooked
certain unifying factors between them which are still more fundamental.

The assigning of relative positions such as "superior" and "inferior" does not, in any case, represent categories which have any
objective justification. That view in which official authority on
the one hand and the community on the other are seen as two
opposite poles, or in which a positive "opposition" between the
two is postulated, does not, in any case, represent the normal relationship between them. A community which has a genuine
spirit of obedience to Jesus Christ will not even wish its leader

to be in a position of *total* dependence upon the community, and only able to "reproduce" that which is already a living force in itself. Certainly the official minister is the spokesman for men with God. But however true this may be, still he also continues to be the prophetic messenger and agent of God who constantly has to contend and remonstrate with man in order to bring him back to heeding the word of God in its pristine and undistorted form.

Unless the word of the Gospel is present as an active force of judgment and correction in the community it is not the community of God at all. Certainly this word does not in all cases, or even primarily, have to come from the Church's official ministers. But there is a further possibility which cannot be excluded. Even after all attempts at reconciliation have been tried out and all rational arguments have been considered it may be, in particular cases and at some particular moment, that a leader of the community finds himself insuperably opposed to individuals, groups or even, in certain circumstances, to the majority of that community. In that case he will have to search his own soul again and again to see whether what he is preaching is his own will or that word of God which still retains its effective and binding force even today. An intervention of the kind we are thinking of in the power of the Gospel may take many forms. But in the context of Christianity it is possible and permitted only in those cases in which the official minister does not speak from his own absolute authority, but rather finds himself compelled to make the voice of Jesus Christ heard in all its fullness, and in which he himself is fulfilling the "ministry of reconciliation" "in the place of Christ" in fear and trembling.

3. *Changes in the Official Ministry and in Authority*

It must be remembered, however, that what this message demands first and foremost is the practical application of an attitude of fellowship, understanding and mutual love. And because of this the first fruits in the relationship between community and official ministry must be an intercourse that is conducted with mutual respect for one another's views, a renunciation of any vain clinging to one's own opinions, and selfless collaboration for the same aims. The more this community effectively binds itself to what is central to its own "basic substance", the more it will liberate itself so as to give an increasing place to working out the problems of living together by means of dialogue and by the removal of all inequalities, provided only that they are such as can be avoided.[25]

If we fully think out this basic attitude, then truly we can only wonder why there should be so few "democratic structures" in the Church in the sense that has been explained. Why do we not already take it completely for granted that much in the style and forms of the Church should be "democratic"? Only in those cases in which no effective and basic agreement in the sense described above has been arrived at, and no continuous and open dialogue has been achieved in conditions of freedom and trust, does the phenomenon arise of insatiable demands being made for a "democratization" of the Church's official ministry. And the motives for these are often merely at the level of a formal legalism or of ecclesiastical politics. The bitterness with which this demand is often pursued and the uncompromising obstinacy with which, not infrequently, it is rejected, betray something of the almost pathological state of affairs in the attitude towards the question of official ministries in the Church, and, moreover, an attitude that is found on all sides.

Democratic awareness must not lead simply to the abolishing of every kind of official authority. It is precisely the oldest, and for the most part the most proved democracies (those of the Anglo-Saxon world) which exhibit a deeply embedded awareness of the necessity and importance of the element of officialdom. Among these it is viewed as a sacred trust in which rights are protected which, of their basic nature, continue to belong to the citizens as trustees.[26] This interpretation of democracy too is aimed at freedom and exercises a critical function in relation to government in that it emphasizes above all the limitations to which

[25] On the question of leading and guiding the community, more detailed observations are to be found in K. Lehmann, "Zur Theologie der Gemeindeleitung", in *Pastoraltheologische Informationen 1970*, ed. by the Conference of German-speaking Pastoral Theologians (Mainz, 1970), pp. 2–31. On the sociological problems involved in the overthrow of existing forms of government cf. also R. Dahrendorf, *Über den Ursprung der Ungleichheit unter den Menschen* (Tübingen, ²1966); *idem, Gesellschaft und Freiheit* (Munich, 1961), pp. 363 ff.

[26] On this cf. W. Hennis, "Amtsgedanke und Demokratiebegriff", in

every kind of "power" is subject and the fact that the way in which it is exercised has to be answered for.

It is precisely when we accord due respect to this kind of interpretation of what democracy means that we see that the official ministries of religion have, even in the conditions arising from ideas and positions belonging to the new age, a perfectly legitimate place in the life of the Church. In this life both the "official" and the "democratic" elements must play their part. In other words it must be lived in the awareness of a task that is shared and with fellowship and brotherhood as the determining factors in it.

VI. The Concrete Form of and the Necessary Conditions for a Process of Democratization in the Church

Christianity has been unable to adopt any "blueprints" from the historical environment of any particular epoch for the forms of its own institutions without profoundly altering them so as to make them correspond to its own specific intentions. For this reason it is not surprising that the same principle applies to the recipe constituted by democracy. At the same time, however, it would be less than candid to suppress the fact that in giving concrete form to the elements in her own constitution, the Church has all along taken advantage to a very considerable extent of secular models and ideas of official administration. It must be admitted that any rigid adherence to the concept of "democratization" is not very meaningful here, for the very reason that no distinctions are drawn within the concept, and also that as a general recipe it is useless.

Nothing is more urgently needed than a *concretization* of the discussion. In order to estimate how far those who seek to promote the *reality* of "democratization in the Church" are contributing to the *real* well-being of the community in doing so, two criteria have to be applied which have received little mention in the literature on the subject up till now:

(1) The demand for democratization in general must be translated into specific and practicable models in which strong priority

Politik als praktische Wissenschaft (Munich, 1968), pp. 48–64, 248–50 (bibliography). The idea, which was applied above in a theological context (cf. V, 2), requires further investigation.

must be given to the problems of how the areas affected of the Church's life can be organized and made functionally efficient and effective.[27]

(2) Anyone who voices the demand for "democratization in the Church" and does not at the same time strive actively to ensure that Christians shall be really and effectively equipped to play an active part in the life and decisions of the community to which they belong in effect brings discredit on his own cause.[28] Unless all members of the particular section of the society involved achieve a greater degree of readiness to share in the responsibilities, the term "democratization" comes all too easily to signify merely the overthrow of "government".

If this orientation towards *specific* aims is borne in mind, then it becomes clear that the very nature of the concept of "democratization" is such that distinctions have to be drawn within it. Unless the general demand is concretized in this way it is hardly possible to achieve any critical evaluation of the many projects and aspirations which are formulated from the aspect of systematic theology. Admittedly there is a certain sense in which the concept has become almost inevitable because in it—and this is something that extends even to the sphere of the emotions—so many hopes and liberalizing movements characteristic of modern man are bound up as it were in a single slogan.[29]

A Church which is intended to have relevance for the men of this age cannot close itself to justifiable demands, and these not merely with regard to subjective states of mind (attitudes, modes of behaviour, etc.), but also with regard to factors which are juridically or institutionally binding. This is especially true in view of the fact that the Church either already has, or else can acquire, in many of her elements an intrinsic affinity with the basic values of democracy.

[27] On this cf. above all Th. Eschenburg, "Demokratisierung und politische Praxis", in *Aus Politik und Zeitgeschichte*. Supplement to the weekly journal, *Das Parliament* 38 (19.9.1970), pp. 3–13, esp. pp. 8 ff., 11 ff.
[28] For a radical treatment cf. G. Zimpel (ed.), *Der beschäftige Mensch. Beiträge zur sozialen und politischen Partizipation* (Politisches Verhalten 1) (Munich, 1970, with bibliography).
[29] On this cf. the memorandum of the Bensberger Circle mentioned in n. 12, pp. 11–22.

Translated by David Bourke

Norbert Greinacher

A Community Free of Rule

MY point of departure for the argument that follows is that a democratization of the Church is urgently required, not in the sense that the rule of those holding office should be replaced by the rule of the people, but rather in the sense that all the members of the Church, in the knowledge that they are committed to their Lord, Jesus Christ, should strive to find a form of life in the Church which is in accordance both with the attitude of their Lord and with those aspects of human thought, behaviour and social order which we call democracy.[1] What is clear from the very beginning is firstly that the democratization both of so-called secular society and of the Church does not imply above all a special, legally established and static social order, but a dynamic process of development. Secondly, the end of this dynamic process of democratization, in other words, full self-determination and discovery of our own identity, is something which we shall never attain in this age, but which we are bound to try to approach more and more closely.

In addition, this process of making the Church more democratic is also something which has to go on taking place at all levels of life within the Church if the Church is to be accepted as credible in a society which is itself involved in a process of fundamental democratization.[2] It would be quite wrong to wait

[1] See, for example, the memorandum of the so-called Bensburg circle: *Die Demokratisierung der Kirche in der Bundesrepublik Deutschland* (Mainz, 1970).
[2] See K. Mannheim, *Mensch und Gesellschaft im Zeitalter des Umbaues* (Darmstadt, 1958).

until the institutions at the higher level of the Church as a whole
—the papacy, the curia, the bishops' synod, episcopal confer-
ences and so on—have become thoroughly democratic. However
important a democratization of these higher institutions may be
and however much serious attention has to be devoted to making
them truly democratic, it is none the less even more important to
begin with the work of democratization at the lowest level, the
basis, of the Church. The local community is the starting-point
for a real democratization of the Church—it is there that a beginning can be made without delay and has, thank God, already
been made in many cases.

If these attempts to develop a democratic attitude and a democratic way of life are successful in the local churches, the institutions at the higher level in the Church as a whole are bound to
take notice of this process. On the other hand, however, any
democratization of the basis is made easier by democratization of
the macrostructures. A "democratic escalation" of this kind can
result in this process developing a special dynamism of its own
and attaining its end—the full democratization of the Church—
asymptotically. But first of all, we must define what is meant by
a church community.

I. What is a Community?

According to the New Testament, the Church takes place
above all in the individual church community. The Church is
not in first place the Church as a whole. On the contrary, what
constitutes the Church becomes an event in the individual community. "The individual church (community) is therefore a
making present and real of the Church as such."[3]

A parish may be a community in the sense in which it is understood here, but it need not necessarily be. It is, for example, possible for several communities to exist within the framework of a
single urban parish, one community for each of the residential
areas. In rural districts, on the other hand, it is possible for
several smaller communities, each representing a village, to
group together to form a single parish. There may also be church

[3] W. Kasper, "Kirche und Gemeinde", in Der Seelsorger, 38 (1968),
pp. 387–93; my quotation from p. 389.

communities which are not tied to any particular territory. Examples of such "functional" communities are university or student societies, Christian family groups, Christian communities in a hospital, large complex of flats or houses or in places of work, and Christian groups whose members belong to a linguistic minority.

If the Church wants to be really close to men and women in all the different spheres of our highly complicated society, then the forms of the individual church communities in which the Church as a whole is realized must above all be flexible, imaginative and adaptable. Christians will also have to get used to the fact that the structures, the way of life and the spiritual orientation of the various church communities will be pluriform. There will, for example, be communities which are more progressively inclined and others which are more conservative in attitude. There will be communities structured, on the one hand, more on the lines of the German "people's church" and, on the other, more on the principle of voluntary activity. Some communities may be more like city "service stations", providing in the first place simply well composed and convincingly celebrated religious services, whereas others may be rather like "effective communities" committed to definite social and political tasks.[4] It is also to be hoped that there will soon be, within the same district, communities some of which have a Roman Catholic tradition and others a Protestant tradition, but all of which recognize each other as communities of Jesus Christ and are integral members of one greater Church.

The church communities can therefore be very different from each other in form and we must be on our guard against any attempt to think of them in a static sense or to force them to fit into a particular pattern. All these pluriform communities, however, have this in common with each other. They represent a group of people who accept the Christian revelation and believe in Jesus Christ, but who also know that this faith in Jesus is also dependent on other believers. These people try to orientate their lives, individually, socially and within the community, towards the message of the New Testament. As members of a Christian

[4] See O. Schreuder, "Die Kirchengemeinden: Typen und Leitbilder", in O. Betz, editor, *Gemeinde von morgen* (Munich, 1969), pp. 53–104.

community, these men and women feel responsible for their community and identify themselves with it. The central point of the life of the community is its regular meeting when the members come together to celebrate the Eucharist. The members regard their community as an integral part of the Church as a whole and know that they are, like Jesus, committed to the service of their fellow men.[5]

II. A COMMUNITY FREE OF RULE

The so-called "New Left", which has been so prominent in student society especially in the West since about 1964, has been subjected to intensive criticism, as indeed have the older philosophers of the movement. It is indeed certainly possible to question both the theory and the practice of this New Left and to ask in particular whether the empirical analyses made by its protagonists do in fact do full justice to the real situation or whether they do not, on the contrary, make so many ideological presuppositions that the way towards a genuine encounter with reality is barred in advance.

One may also ask whether the plans made by the New Left for the world of the future can really be carried out at all or whether they are not just as dogmatically rigid and inflexible as the structures of present-day society which the members of the movement so sharply criticize. Finally, it is even possible to wonder whether the ideology of the New Left does not ultimately lead to the very violation and alienation in human society that the members themselves attack so strenuously and so rightly. In spite of this, however, this movement has one undeniable merit. Its members have compelled at least some of us in the "free Western world" to examine this "freedom" critically. They have made us more alert to the fact that man's rule or power over other men is not always exercised in such spectacularly brutal and inhuman ways as it was by fascist and Nazi regimes using torture, racial persecution and concentration camps. Man can also rule over his fellow men in more refined, secret and cunning ways, which are hidden from the gaze of most men, and

[5] See N. Greinacher, "Leitbild einer kirchlichen Gemeinde von morgen", in *Theologie der Gegenwart*, 12 (1969), pp. 212–19.

this form of rule, which is used both in capitalist and in socialist societies, is extremely effective and ultimately just as inhuman as the more notorious methods.

We are bound to agree with the protagonists of the New Left—man rules over his fellow men not only in socialist societies and in the developing countries, but also in industrialized, capitalist societies. The capitalist West also has social instruments by means of which force is exercised in secret but very effective ways and in a perhaps unspectacular but extremely inhuman manner and it possesses unjust and repressive structures which are used to exploit men, alienate them and do violence to them.

In this, we can take as our point of departure the distinction made by H. Marcuse: "Rule is different from the rational exercise of power. The latter, which is inherent to every division of labour that forms society, is derived from ability and is confined to the administration of the functions and institutions that are necessary to the advancement of the whole. In contrast to this, the rule of a certain group or of certain individuals is exercised with the intention of maintaining oneself in a privileged position and of increasing one's power".[6] In our society, there is, on the one hand, the "additional oppression" which consists of limitations that are necessary in order to preserve man's rule over his fellow men. This is different from, on the other hand, "the (fundamental) oppression, the modification of impulse which is indispensable for the continued existence of the human race in society".[7]

As Christians, we have therefore to ask ourselves honestly— what is the real situation now and what has it been in the past with regard to this rule or power in the Church? Even if we leave aside the notorious and inhuman cases of the official exercise of power in the past, such as witch hunts, the burning of heretics and the abuse of indulgences, there still remain many other questions which we are bound to ask ourselves as Christians if only because they are being put to the Church today with increasing urgency and clarity. Has, for example, the form of education evolved by the Church not in fact very often produced the authoritarian type of personality that is the prerequisite for the

[6] *Triebstruktur und Gesellschaft* (Frankfurt, 1970), p. 41.
[7] *Op. cit.*, p. 40.

exercise of power? Has the threat of "pain of mortal sin" not all too frequently given rise to a fear and anxiety which is in itself inhuman and at the same time made man's rule over his fellow men much easier? Has the confessional perhaps not been open to abuse as an instrument of power over others? Has the Church's teaching about sex not led in many cases to alienation and therefore to a relationship of dependence which does violence to human dignity?

Certainly, one would have to be on one's guard against giving premature answers to these and similar questions and it would be necessary to analyse with great care the situations in which these structures have been employed in the past to ascertain whether or not they have been consciously and explicitly abused by those holding office in the Church in order to exercise power over others or whether they have simply developed to the point where they have become *de facto* instruments in the stabilization of positions of power.

It would also be necessary to ask whether certain phenomena in the background of the historical and social situation at various periods could hardly have occurred differently. In other words, we Christians are undeniably bound to ask ourselves repeatedly and to examine critically and honestly again and again whether and to what extent power has been exercised in the Church, despite the appalling fact that the Church is subject to an entirely different law: "You know that those who are supposed to rule over the Gentiles lord it over them, and their great men exercise authority over them. But it shall not be so among you; but whoever would be great among you must be your servant, and whoever would be first among you must be slave of all. For the Son of Man also came not to be served but to serve, and to give his life as a ransom for many" (Mark 10. 42–45).

The way in which authority and power has been exercised by those holding office in the Church and by Christians generally in the past and is still exercised in the present has to be measured and judged according to this unequivocal and indeed severe norm and any rule over others in the sense of "lording it" over them— even a sacred rule or "hierarchy"—must be condemned. It may perhaps be that, in the past, mankind, including the Church, was not mature enough to manage without exercising this kind of power. But nowadays, in a world that has finally come of age, it is certainly necessary to achieve a situation in the Church which is at last fully in accordance with the basic structure of service to others that was taught by Jesus in all that he said and in the example of his own life and death.

The place where the Church becomes a concrete event, however, is the individual community of the Church. The one Lord whom the community of Jesus Christ professes is the Lord Jesus Christ. The recognition of his authority, to which all other authority in the Church has to be subject, by his community does not, however, in any way imply an exercise of power or rule in the sense outlined above, because Jesus himself saw his task as a service to others. There should not even be paternal authority in the community of Jesus and certainly not a patriarchal authority (see Matt. 23. 8–12).

If the Church—and this of course means, in the concrete, the local church community—wants to be accepted as credible, however, then it must be a community that is free of rule. This does not mean that it is to be a community without any exercise of power in the true sense, without any order or authority or without anyone placed in authority, a community handed over to chaos and anarchy. It means that, if power is exercised in the community by certain people holding office, this must be a responsible power. I shall be returning to this later.

A community that is free of rule is a community which takes very seriously the reality proclaimed by Jesus as the rule or kingdom of God. The special characteristic of this rule or kingdom of God, which has been brought closer to us in the person of Jesus, is that man is not once again made subject to a rule, but is, on the contrary, made free so long as he accepts Jesus. The kingdom of God which is proclaimed and brought to us by Jesus is the condition which makes human freedom possible. "For freedom Christ has set us free; stand fast therefore, and do not submit again to the yoke of slavery" (Gal. 5. 1). The event of Christ has an enormously liberating, redeeming and dynamic effect. "Everyone should be free enough to live as a man. This affirmation deprived those who were ruling at the time of Jesus of one of their means of ruling and exercising power—their appeal to God. If Jesus talks and acts in this way and men take it seriously and respond to it, not letting themselves be deceived any longer about their freedom and human dignity, then, in Jesus' view, a change of rule is in sight. Men are liberated by good, set free to do good. In this, a reality seizes hold of power, a reality which is the only one that has the right to rule over men and their world. This reality is the one that is to be found under the name of God."[8]

This reality, which in the first place concerns the individual who accepts the Christian revelation and believes in Jesus Christ and which sets him free from the "principalities and powers", must of necessity also have consequences for man's life together with other men and, again in the first place, for the community of the Church which is a community of free men. All the various differences which are important in human society as a whole—nationality, race, social position, sex and so on—are no longer valid in the Church community: "There is neither Jew nor Greek, there is neither slave nor free, there is neither male nor female; for you are all one in Christ Jesus" (Gal. 3. 28). "In the Church of Christ, there are no power structures in the sense that new positions of dependence or subordination are created or that a Christian society of two unequal classes comes about. . . . Power of this kind would amount to fundamental contempt for human freedom and consequently contempt for the Gospel."[9]

Furthermore, this freedom of the children of God and this community of the Church as the community of free men must also radiate an effect on human society as a whole—this is something to which I shall return later.

Jesus Christ has overcome man's alienation. In Jesus Christ, God has "delivered us from the dominion of darkness and transferred us to the kingdom of his beloved Son" (Col. 1. 13). He has set us free, enabling us to live freely in a way that is worthy of men. Jesus is himself the most perfect and the most fortunate and happy of men, because the most fundamental encounter between God and man has taken place in him. If all this is true, then the community of Christians must also be a truly human community. We are bound to say in all honesty that the Church

[8] K. Schäfer, "Nochmals: Zum Thema Priestergruppen", in *Stimmen der Zeit*, 185 (1970), pp. 361–78, my quotation p. 367; see also M. Raske and others, editors, *Eine freie Kirche für eine freie Welt* (Düsseldorf, 1969).

[9] J. Blank, *Das Evangelium als Garantie der Freiheit* (Würzburg, 1970), p. 44.

has often enough in history not pleaded the cause of humanity. "The history of Christian freedom has been, in this sense, a way of the cross, at which the Churches are bound to look back more with shame than with pride."[10]

It is a cause of dismay that the community of free men has all too frequently been a community without freedom and lacking in basic humanity, spreading fear and anxiety among men, and that in modern times Christians have by no means always been the first to espouse the cause of liberty, equality and fraternity. "With the declaration of human rights and its insistence on the basic human freedoms, contemporary society is clearly quite a long way ahead of the Church. The same applies to the development of law, in which society is more Christian than the existing Churches."[11] The struggle for the recognition of human dignity has taken place outside the Church. In fact, the Church has even opposed this struggle, without apparently realizing that it was her own flesh and blood that was involved. It is urgently necessary for the Church to recognize this illegitimate child as her own grown-up son and for her to give a home and a true welcome to humanity in the fullest sense. We should, after all, not accept simply without question the fact that not only our non-Christian contemporaries, but also members of the Church themselves should feel our Church to be lacking in freedom and in basic humanity. Surely the Church and, in the concrete, every Christian community should be the place where something of the "goodness and loving-kindness of God our Saviour appears" (Tit. 3. 4) and from which something of man's basic humanity is radiated.

Whenever Christians gather together as a community under the name of Jesus, they should not only appear more redeemed, but also really be redeemed, set free, happy and human. There are too many forms of humanity in the Church and at the same time too little fundamental humanity. It must be made clearly visible in the Church that there is concern for people, their salvation, their welfare and their happiness. This concern must be seen in the meetings of the church community for worship and work together, in the way in which all the members of the community associate with each other, in the relationships between the

[10] E. Käsemann, *Der Ruf der Freiheit* (Tübingen, [3]1968), p. 54.
[11] J. Blank, *op. cit.*, pp. 45 f.

members and those holding office and between the various groups within the community as a whole. Our contemporaries must be able to see that "the joy and hope, grief and anxiety of people today, especially of poor and oppressed people, is also the joy and hope, grief and anxiety of the disciples of Christ".[12] It should be clear to them that the cares and problems, distress and unhappiness, difficulties and suffering and desires and needs of all mankind are seen in the Church community and taken seriously by its members. They must be able to recognize that members of all Christian communities feel at one with humanity and are concerned to bring about the *terre des hommes* about which Saint-Exupéry wrote.

III. CHARACTERISTICS OF THE COMMUNITY THAT IS FREE OF RULE

1. *The Collegial Responsibility of All Members of the Community*

In the view of many Christians today, an image of the Church has almost imperceptibly evolved, an image which can perhaps best be characterized by the term "client Church". This concept points to a way of regarding the Church as another institution existing in order to provide a definite service, rather like an insurance society, a sales organization or a company handling investments. According to this view, the Church is above all the men holding office, the clergy, and these officials have the task of taking care of the members and have always to be on call, ready to officiate whenever they are needed—at births, deaths and marriages and perhaps also whenever, for example, a building or a bridge has to be blessed or a special festival celebrated. For the rest, however, they are expected to leave the members of the Church strictly alone. "The client mentality is closely connected with the patriarchal and feudal structures of the Church which have prevailed up to the present time and within which the active participation of the members of the Church has been minimal."[13]

[12] See the Pastoral Constitution, *Gaudium et Spes*, on the Church in the Modern World, n. 1.
[13] E. Golomb. "Kirchenstruktur und Brüderlichkeit heute", in H. Erharter and E. Hesse, editors, *Koinonia. Kirche und Brüderlichkeit* (Vienna, 1968), pp. 47–65, my quotation from p. 63.

A patriarchal attitude and brotherly love are, however, mutually exclusive and it is high time that this patriarchal attitude, which is both sociologically out of date and essentially unchristian. was done away with in the community of Jesus Christ. According to Matt. 22. 8, there cannot be a patriarchal rule in the Christian community—there can only be collegial solidarity and brotherly love. The Christian community can no longer be a parish family in the old sense, with the parish priest, "Father", determining everything that is to take place in his family and ruling with patriarchal authority over his "children". It must be a mature community of brothers and sisters who have come of age. Even the idea of the pastor or "shepherd", despite its undeniably biblical foundation, is no longer really adequate to our present situation, because the necessary complement to the shepherd is the sheep and nobody wants to be thought of as sheep today.

The basic principle of the Christian community that is free of such rule must therefore be that of the collegial responsibility of all the members of the community. All the members of the Church community have to be co-responsible for the carrying out of the life of the community. "Gathered together as one in the people of God and included in the one body of Christ under one head, the lay people, whoever they may be, are called, as living members, to devote all the powers that they have received from the generosity of their creator and the grace of their redeemer to the growth and the increasing sanctification of the Church."[14]

Within the Christian community, all members are not only entitled but also obliged to contribute to the building up of the body of Christ (see Eph. 4. 12). There cannot be, nor should there be, a society of two classes in the Christian community, a society of rulers and ruled, a society of priests and lay people. It may be that the concept "laity" should even be gradually buried in the Church, because there are, basically, no more lay people in the sense in which this term has currently been used, that is to say, in the sense of non-specialist. All members of the Christian community understand something of the community and the way in which its life is carried out. As there is no basis in the New Testament for a sociological evaluation of the social status

[14] See the Dogmatic Constitution, *Lumen gentium*, on the Church, n. 33.

of clergy and laity and their consequent separation into two distinct social categories, this must inevitably be regarded as very questionable.

We cannot, however, speak of co-responsibility on the part of all the members of the Christian community if we do not give these members the right and the opportunity to share in the making of decisions. If this right is not granted, there is a great risk that any appeal to share in the responsibility and the work of the community will be interpreted as hypocritical. It is only when all the members of the community are allowed to share in the making of decisions that it will be possible for all these Christians to be fully integrated into the community and to identify themselves with it—in other words, when they see that it is really their own community, in the sense of their having something effective to say in it.

This collegial responsibility of all the members of the Christian community for the life of that community has, moreover, to be expressed institutionally in what I should prefer to call a community synod, that is, a body which is elected by all the members, which enjoys their full confidence and which collaborates closely and in trust with the leader of the community and makes the task of caring for the life of the community its own. The "parish councils" which have been set up recently in many church communities are a first step in this direction, but a great deal more has to be done to make them really democratically effective. A body which is only partly the result of an election and which possesses no more than a consultative power is very far indeed from the model of the Christian community found in the New Testament and reformulated in the Second Vatican Council. The inevitable consequence of the persistence of this type of body without further development is the emergence of the serious suspicion that an alibi has been created under the illusion of democracy for the continued existence in the Church of the old authoritarian structures.

It is, of course, true that there are several different types of structure to be found in the New Testament for the Christian community, but even in the pastoral letters, in which the office of the leader of the community is outlined very clearly, this office is fully integrated into the principle of collegiality. In our present situation, the credibility of the Christian community will to a very great extent depend on whether the community shows itself to be responsible in its synod and its leader and whether it has an active share in determining the way in which the communal life is led.

2. Publicity in the Community

The public character of the older patriarchal church community was purely representative, in that the community was represented in the figure of the parish priest. He could say, with a certain justice, *"La paroisse, c'est moi"*.[15] A community is, however, public in the sense in which I am using the term here only if it at least potentially allows all its members to see what is taking place inside it.[16] (It should be noted in passing that I do not use the word "publicity" purely in its modern commercial sense of "advertising".) If we take really seriously the theological affirmation that all members of the Christian community are responsible for the life of the Church and that the promise to send the Spirit of Christ was made to the whole Church, then the community is bound to guarantee that all its proceedings will be made public. It will simply not be possible to hold, as it were, secret cabinet meetings to decide on policy. The member of the community can no longer be expected to guess what the leader who holds office in the Church has decided in his goodness and wisdom. He will inevitably share in the decisions made about all questions relating to the life of the community. An efficient and comprehensive pattern of communications is, however, the prerequisite for real publicity in the community. The life of the community is sustained by the constant interchange of communication between all its members.

So far, however, almost the only communication which has taken place in the community has been from above to below and, generally speaking, the handing on of information, directives, admonitions and so on from the parish priest down to the parishioners has functioned quite well. But the real weakness of this flow of communication, of course, has always been that it

[15] See J. Habermas, *Strukturwandel der Öffentlichkeit* (Neuwied, ⁴1969).
[16] See H. P. Bahrdt, *Die moderne Grossstadt* (Hamburg, 1969), especially pp. 58–95.

was only a one-way traffic—there has hardly ever been any flow in the opposite direction from below to above. Yet it is precisely communication in this direction which is so important—information, criticism, wishes and suggestions must be transmitted from individual members of the community to the leadership. In addition, there must also be a steady flow of communication between the members themselves.

Certain safeguards will, of course, have to be taken to prevent the occurrence of a purely illusory publicity in the community. This can often come about when the members of the community behave as though publicity existed in their community, but when in fact this publicity is manipulated by an individual member or by a small group with the conscious or unconscious intention of preserving a position of power, under the cloak, of course, of democratic conduct.

Another danger of publicity in the community is that of violating the privacy of the members. The community should above all not become a totalitarian system. This does not, of course, mean that every member should simply do as he pleases at his own discretion. It means rather that there is great individual responsibility exercised in common, a responsibility to which common consent, based on an understanding of the content of Christian faith, is given. In a sense, the community has to allow the individual to express himself freely in the sphere of individual privacy, because it is only a sphere of individual privacy which can really guarantee a sphere of publicity in the community and vice versa.

If this sphere of publicity in the community really exists, then criticism can also be publicly expressed. A totalitarian system cannot permit criticism of itself, because this questions its claim to be a total and absolute institution. The Christian community should, it goes without saying, be an open institution which is dependent on the collaboration and co-responsibility of all of its members and an institution of this kind can be positively nourished by the criticism of its members. The very guarantee of the dynamism and flexibility of the community is this positive criticism, which can at the same time also encourage the members to continue to work towards increasing perfection in the life of the community.

If this criticism is to be really effective, it has to be given to some extent an institutional form. What is needed, in other words, is a legitimate opposition in the community. This means that certain groups of people not only have to be tolerated in the Church—they are also extremely necessary. These are, of course, the groups which examine the existing institution of the Church critically and wherever necessary press for its reform. It would be fatal if the less vocally critical members of the Christian community were to act as though these groups—or individuals within these groups—lacked faith or good intentions just because they were bold enough to express criticism. If they were forced out of the Church, the community would undoubtedly have lost one of its most necessary and dynamic elements.

The same applies to other minorities in the community. The growing pluriformity in society as a whole is accompanied by an increasing pluriformity of opinions in the Christian community. It is no longer possible to speak of *the* Catholic point of view in every question. What must now happen in this case is that the church community should be the living example, on the basis of its Christian understanding of faith, of respect for minorities and of close co-operation with them. It must be possible, in the Christian community, for disputes and disagreements to be settled in an honest way and in public. They should never be suppressed or concealed.

There will inevitably be decisions of a more organizational nature in the community which are made by the majority and have to be respected by the minority. If, however, it has to do with fundamental questions of Christian faith and its realization in the world of today, it will be less possible to come to a decision by means of a simple majority vote. In such cases, either compulsion has to be used to obtain agreement between those of opposing views or else the question has to be left open. Any presumptuous attempt on the part of a person holding office in the community to force a decision in such open questions can only be the result of a fundamental contempt for the Church's consciousness of faith. To leave questions open is no more than going back to an ancient practice in the Church which was based on the conviction that a theologically disputed question could not be decided by the Church's teaching office.

3. Office in the Community

According to the New Testament (especially, for example, I Cor. 12 and Rom. 12), there are, in the community of Jesus Christ, many different services to be fulfilled if the community is to accomplish its mission. These services are carried out by individual members of the community in accordance with their abilities and their charismatic gifts. It is therefore of great importance that these abilities and gifts should be discovered and recognized by the community and one often has the impression that abilities and gifts of this kind, which could be put at the service of the community, are far more common among members of the community, especially among the women members, than is generally supposed.

One service among the many services of the community is that of the priest. The priestly office of leadership should serve the peace and unity of the community. The leader of the community has the task of detecting the gifts that may be used in the service of the community, of giving them sufficient scope and encouragement, of co-ordinating them, relating them meaningfully to each other and, wherever necessary, also calling them to order. On the one hand, the priestly office of leadership is directed towards the community and, on the other, it is orientated in service towards Christ, the Lord of that community. That is why, in carrying out his service to the community, the leader is in a certain sense placed in confrontation with his community and cannot, as it were, simply be derived from that community. He has the task of presiding at the celebration of the sacraments and above all at the celebration of the Eucharist. He is also especially responsible for the task of proclaiming the Christian message, although he is admittedly not the only one who is responsible for this.

If the leader is really to enjoy the confidence of the community, it is most important for him to be elected in collaboration with the community and perhaps even, in certain cases, to be called from the ranks of the community itself. If this were to be done, it would be no more than a revival of a very old Christian tradition and one which has, moreover, continued in a few places uninterrupted up to the present.

Another very important question is the co-ordination and division of authority between the leader of the community, the community synod and the community as a whole. There is no doubt that there will have to be a great deal of experimentation here. But, as a fundamental principle, the obligation and, in many cases, the absolute need to co-operate is bound to hold good. This is a principle which has long been put into practice in so-called secular spheres of society generally and has often been surrounded, at least in part, by legal safeguards.

This means, in our case, that of the Church, that the leader, the synod and the community as a whole have to co-operate with each other and that, because of this mutual dependence, decisions will not normally be taken without the consent of all these groups. There is, for example, no authority in marriage which can intervene in cases of conflict—the husband and wife are dependent on each other for mutual agreement or disagreement. The situation is analogous with regard to the relationship between the leader of the Christian community, the community synod and the community as a whole. They are all predisposed towards co-operation. They are all interdependent and none can make a decision without the other. This principle can also be institutionalized, so that the right of veto may even be accorded to the leader or a minority in especially difficult questions. In very difficult cases of conflict—which should, after all, be exceptional in a Christian community—there should be a court of arbitration at least at diocesan level and this court would attempt to solve such conflicts.

Those who are placed in a position of power in a democratic society have again and again to justify their exercise of that power before the tribunal of individual and collective reason. In the same way, it is also necessary for those holding office in the Christian community to justify the structures of the institution of their office and the way in which they exercise power in the light of the message of Christ and the living faith of the Church. This is because there is always a tendency, frequently latent but therefore all the more dangerous, for those in office to forget that their office is above all a service to others, to isolate themselves from the main body of believers, to make themselves absolute and to overlook the fact that their office is always subordinate to and always refers back to the message of Christ. It is precisely for these reasons that it is so necessary to justify the office of the priesthood by referring it constantly to the word of God and to the Church's understanding of faith.

In the Church, the man who holds and carries out an office is of necessity also exercising power. This exercise of power, however, always presents a problem. There is always a danger that a legitimate, necessary and rational exercise of power will become man's rule over his fellow men. According to the New Testament, however, the exercise of power in the Church should have a specific character. It is subject to a fundamental norm: "Whoever would be first among you must be slave of all" (Mark 10. 44). Power has therefore to be exercised in the Christian community in accordance with this saying of Christ, but no one would ever claim that this has always been the case or even that it is so nowadays. Even now, the exercise of power in the Church is understood far too frequently in the light of the "hierarchy", the rule which is all the more dangerous because it claims to be a holy or sacred rule, based on faith, but alas all too often exerting a repressive influence under the cloak of a religious ideology. In the face of this kind of attitude, it is urgently necessary for all of those in office in the Church to go back again and again to the Gospel to consider the way in which they should exercise power.

In addition to this, it is also most important constantly to check and verify this exercise of power in the Christian community and, in this, the Pauline teaching about office in the Church is of course indispensable. The community has, Paul tells us, to judge what is said by the prophets (1 Cor. 14. 29). In 1 Thess. 5. 21, he defines a universal principle: "Test everything; hold fast to what is good, abstain from every form of evil". There is also invaluable teaching in the Johannine letters: "Do not believe every spirit, but test the spirits to see whether they are of God" (1 John 4. 1). The Christian community is therefore clearly exhorted to judge critically all that is said and done even in questions of faith and to do this with all the members of the community in mind, including the one holding office.

It is also extremely important that any decisions which have to be made in the Church community are taken in a fully democratic way and in faithfulness to the message of Christ. It would be wrong to do no more than simply to publicize the decisions made by the one in office in the community. The aim should rather be to inform the community fully about the problems that have to be dealt with, to do everything possible to sound opinions among the members of the community and to present the results to the community synod for discussion. The existence of publicity and means of communication in the community is essential to this process of making decisions. Above all, decisions about questions that are of great importance to the life of the community should never be made unilaterally by the one holding office. They must be made in co-operation with the whole community.

Every attempt has, therefore, to be made to take important decisions of this kind in the most practical and business-like manner possible. As far as the community is concerned, this means that the criteria for these decisions have to be based on the norm of the Christian message and at the same time on the existing situation in society. The ultimate decisions taken by those empowered to do so have therefore to be made on the basis of all these various considerations. Finally, it should be mentioned that experts should, wherever possible, be consulted and their co-operation enlisted in this process of making important decisions concerning the life of the Christian community.

4. *The Relative Autonomy of the Community*

If it is true to say that the Church becomes an event above all in the individual community of Christians, then it follows that each individual community must also possess a certain independence. Just as the national Churches and the individual dioceses are in urgent need of a certain independence from the Roman Curia, so too do the individual communities need independence from the episcopal "Curia". Above all, the Church is hindered today by its extremely centralized structure. This centralization cannot be justified on the basis of the New Testament, nor can it be vindicated in the light of the contemporary situation in society. It is based purely on the idea of an absolute monarchy. It is undeniable, as far as the practical life of the Church is concerned, that the individual communities must have freedom from this centralized structure if they are to develop properly.

This freedom or autonomy is, of course, bound to be a relative independence. Each individual community must, in other words, recognize that it is intimately related to the other Christian communities and to the Church as a whole. If this relationship is not acknowledged, there is always a great danger that sects will come about. This relationship between the individual communities and the Church as a whole has to be based on the principle of subsidiarity. The individual communities have to decide, on their own responsibility, what they can do on the basis of their own abilities and the possibilities open to them. On the other hand, however, they must also always be available to co-operate with other communities and to place their authorities and organs at the disposal of others or of the Church as a whole whenever this is required by the situation or by the nature of the problem. Conversely, the Church as a whole has above all the task of serving the local Christian communities and the individual believer.

Each individual community is also dependent on the help of the other communities. There is even reference in the New Testament to the financial help given by some local communities to others (Rom. 15. 26). But, over and above this purely financial assistance, it is necessary for communities to be in communication with each other so that they can strengthen each other in faith now as they did in biblical times (see, for example, Acts 14. 22). "However important the individual communities may be, they should on no account be regarded as isolated monads. What applies within the individual community is also applicable to the relationship between all the communities: 'there should be no discord in the body, but all the members should have the same care for one another. If one member suffers, all suffer together; if one member is honoured, all rejoice together' (1 Cor. 12. 25 f.)."[17] Individual communities can also perform a mutual service by criticizing each other so that there is no need for any community to run into a blind alley. It is certainly true that "anti-criticism forms an integral part of all criticism, because not everything that sounds critical has to be accepted uncritically as correct. The Church can only be what she claims to be as a unity in plurality

[17] F. Klostermann, *Prinzip Gemeinde* (Vienna, 1965), p. 78.

—*signum et sacramentum unitatis*, the sign and sacrament of unity for the world (Dogmatic Constitution, *Lumen gentium*, on the Church)."[18]

CONCLUSION

If Christians really succeed in establishing communities that are free of rule in this way, the Church will almost certainly become credible again in contemporary society. She may also do more and perhaps even evolve models of democratic behaviour and activity which will provide an example to so-called secular society. Instead of continuing to run the risk of being one of the few surviving relics of feudalism in a democratic environment, the Church may become herself democratic in a most exemplary way and thus be able to carry out her critical function in society. This will, of course, take a long time, but it is encouraging to see how many Christians are concerned with the task of building up such communities and how their number is increasing. To undertake this task, we need what Karl Rahner has called the "tutiorism of risk"[19] and we need to experience and experiment in the way that Augustine described, *"Nos autem in experimentis volvimur"*. H. Schmidt has interpreted this as "We are driven by the events of the age we live in from trial to trial, from experience to experience and from experiment to experiment".[20]

[18] W. Kasper, "Kirche und Gemeinde", *op. cit.*, p. 392.
[19] K. Rahner, "Löschet den Geist nicht aus", in *Schriften zur Theologie*, VII (Einsiedeln, 1966), pp. 77–90.
[20] H. Schmidt, *Vita experimentalis* (Munich, 1959), p. 9.

Translated by N. D. Smith

Jean Remy

The Diffusion of Information in the Church: A Way Out of the Unequal Dialogue?

Introduction

THE right to information is nowadays looked on as a condition of participation. Some innovating groups see this as a means for getting out of the unequal dialogue; others see it as a possible way of getting rid of ambiguities and fostering better understanding; all think it would bring about a development in horizontal and vertical communication that would be favourable to any dynamic group. Publicity, in the sense of information available to everyone about everything, would then be a means of re-establishing contact where there has been a breakdown in communication.

The sociologist sees this image of perfect transparency in the context of daily life where it forces itself on the spontaneous consciousness of certain groups. In his observation it is thus fitting that he should make a preliminary move to break things down so as to find out who are the users of this guiding-image—centred on perfect transparency as a condition of ideal social life—and what are the consequences of its use for social life, including the life of the Church. For instance, does this guiding-image contribute towards a sound analysis of situations or does it obscure them? Does it enable us to analyse the causes of the breakdown in communication and, if it is necessary to get out of the unequal dialogue, does it enable us to recognize the causes of the latter, at least those that have social origins?

With regard to the problem of sociological analysis, we shall try simply to introduce a certain way of asking questions. In any case this introduction to the subject will remain very fragmentary and generalized given the framework granted it here.

I. "Perfect Transparency" as Legitimizing Image

Perfect transparency, as the ideal statute governing information, postulates a situation wherein each person has equal opportunities for acquiring and giving information concerning decisions taken at all levels of social life. Some people see this as enabling harmonious relationships to be re-established. For from this starting-point the masses, now informed, would no longer put false interpretations on the reactions of authority; while authority, knowing better the needs of the masses, would not risk reacting inadequately even with the best of intentions. Thus, through improvement in communication, harmonious relations could be re-established with regard to the hierarchy. For the people who see things this way, this means that the breakdown of communication, and the resulting oppositions, have a psycho-sociological origin and that in consequence an improvement in communication—by means of the spread of information—would bring about in the life of large groups the rediscovery of a situation similar to the one obtaining in small groups that function correctly.

For other people, however, the problem lies elsewhere. Perfect transparency serves as an image for the application of a democratic ideal, achieving equality in the realm of information. The various facilities at the disposal of authority for gathering information are not at the disposal of those at the bottom to the same extent, and as a result those at the bottom are deprived of, or at any rate restricted in, their capacity to react. On the other hand authority, under the seal of secrecy, can take decisions enabling it to direct the group in virtue of aims not spontaneously accepted by those at the bottom. People of this trend of opinion ask why, if the aims of authority coincide with the aims of those at the bottom, authority should try to hide them. So, for this group, the right to information implies a modification of the power-relationship, and would enable those at the bottom—largely due to the mediation of public opinion—to get out of the unequal dialogue.

In this perspective, oppositions and conflicts cannot be resolved by an improvement in communication reintroducing harmonious interpersonal relationships. We know that, even if a type of inter-personal relationship is viewed as being important for re-estab-lishing dialogue, these conflicts find their primary origin elsewhere and particularly in a different concept of what is con-sidered best for the future of the group. Thus, for instance, we see a group defending a more "conflictive" ideal society and putting forward the fact that it is from conflict that new creations arise; this concept is based on the sentiment that it is the totality of the members of the group that decides the group's orientation and that thus support should properly be sought here. Now, recourse to public opinion presupposes that, in the view of the group, it is possible for conflict to arise between those at the bottom and the organization that represents them, for example between Nation and State, and this involves the right to express public criticism of the organization in organs explicitly provided for this end, in-dependently of the reactions of those elected to represent the people. Used in this way the concept takes on different mean-ings: it allows the legitimization of reactions to a breakdown whose primary origin does not lie on the psycho-sociological plane or on the plane of reciprocal inadequate information, and it backs up a will to get out of the unequal dialogue by giving to those at the bottom the elements they need to make a judgment.

Can such a concept be applied to the internal life of the Church so as to improve her dynamism as a community? That is a ques-tion to which analysts can make no answer. It can merely observe whether there are groups within the Church that share the same point of view.

From what we have said there emerges first and foremost the fact that the image of perfect transparency is a legitimizing image (that is to say one that can serve as foundation for the legitimacy of certain demands for change), but that—like all legitimizing images—this one can be used in different ways, as its social effi-cacy does not depend on its precise character such as one would expect from a scientific concept of analysis.

II. UTOPIAN CHARACTERISTICS OF THIS IDEALIZED IMAGE

A. *It has served as reference for the classical and rationalistic orientation in the theory of decision*

First we must notice a homology between this image and the

economic theories of perfect competition which presuppose that all the producers and consumers know the conditions of the market and are able to judge for themselves the quality of the product. This situation in no way excludes the development of an unequal relationship. Equality exists only in so far as the producer and consumer are in a so-called "atomistic" situation, that is to say a situation where each has only an infinitesimal influence on the whole. Hence the emergence of a tendency to set out not from dominant groups but from the sum of individual reactions.

This simplified situation may permit an elaboration of the line of argument, but it is not necessarily a schematization allowing an approach to adequate decision-taking in concrete situations. This construction can be made the other way round in relation to the habitual development of economic life. The image of perfect transparency has also contributed to working out the classical and rationalistic orientation in the theory of decision. Here each person is seen as an individual agent choosing in full consciousness between the various alternatives by which he is confronted— because he is able to calculate the consequences of his decision in relation to the aims that he sets himself. This theory creates the illusion that in the normal evolution of social life there is a condition of transparency and a minimal bond between the individual and the group. Most recent theories show that a realistic way to analyse decision-taking should start from an almost opposite hypothesis.[1] One of the problems to be solved by social life, and particularly by organizations, is that of avoiding—or finding ways of reducing—uncertainty. So one will readily adopt the first satisfactory solution, that is to say the one that least upsets the known universe in which we live. On the other hand a condition of perfect knowledge would not be the best possible one if it multiplied areas of uncertainty. Thus, for a large number of decisions, one cannot foresee the consequences. Is not one of the essential problems of authority to react as quickly as possible to unforeseen consequences? It is also to be noted that a faulty initial evaluation sometimes favours decision-taking, while previous awareness of the difficulties produces reluctance to take

[1] "Vers une nouvelle théorie de la décision" by Catherine Gremion (*Sociologie du Travail*, 1969, No. 4, pp. 463–71).

the risk. Thus the opacity within which choices operate can be a condition by means of which new things are undertaken.

At this point the analyst is helping to make explicit the *processus* whereby collective changes and the choices of social agents are effectively made: how does the agent react from within an environment whence proceed a good number of his preferences and possibilities of action? From this angle the role of information is reintroduced, but the attitude is more critical than the one aroused by spontaneous consciousness in virtue of perfect transparency.

B. *The control of information as condition of the life of a group*

Many elements could go to show how simple, not to say inadequate, is an image of perfect transparency for thinking out the problems of social life. We shall confine ourselves to an example linked to the conditions of group development. A group is based on the creation between its members of internal solidarities superior to external solidarities. Moreover, these solidarities are forged by aims which the group is able to pursue but which are superior to the sum of the aims that each member could undertake individually. This internal loyalty means that a number of things are said within the group that will not be repeated in the same way outside it. Thus, for instance, a fringe group can claim the right to clandestinity, that is the right to have contacts within itself, and yet—even with a very weak social visibility— it can simultaneously claim authority's obligation to inform it as to conditions in decision-taking. An inverse but similar strategy can be found on the side of authority when it arrogates to itself the right to take autonomous decisions, that is decisions surrounded by a certain secrecy, while demanding that others should have an attitude of total openness towards it—thus tending to incriminate groups at the bottom when they have reserves about this openness. In both cases we are dealing with parallel lines of strategy: it is in a group's interest to keep part of the information at its disposal hidden, but it seeks to increase its possibilities of intervention by maximal knowledge of the context and by opposing the constitution of counter-groups which would have their area of social non-visibility. It follows that the achievement of perfect transparency would result in suppressing the development of social life through group action But we are well aware that it is only through and by means of groups that certain aims will be able to be pursued. A universe of perfect transparency, then, implies in practice a very individualistic universe in which group life and development are at a great disadvantage. It is not in this way that collective changes are accomplished and certainly not changes concerned with culture. A multiplicity of ungovernable elements intervene, the more so as these changes do not depend solely on organized groups but on social movements that are collective processes with structures that are less apparent, though not necessarily less permanent. Furthermore, these social movements give scope for inner identifications within their members which allow for frank discussion between people considered trustworthy, and despite the absence of explicitly constituted groups each sifts out the information given to the outside world.

This analysis of the utopian character of the concepts of transparency and the right to information, as obtaining in social life, has meaning only in so far as these concepts are operative for transforming certain power-relationships. Our intention is to examine their capacity as guide-lines in relation to their capacity to obscure the issue, while not denying their power to legitimize and make claims.

An analysis of these concepts is all the more important as the control and regulation of communications has become a central problem for societies based on information. This control is decisive not only for organizations having large-scale social functions but also for the ordinary citizen who has to react in a world of multiple and complex information and who should thus be in a position to select. This is a characteristic regarded by some writers as being of the essence of "urbanization",[2] that is to say of the citizen capable of using in a positive way the urbanized context into which we are entering. Hence the regulation of the way in which information is circulated and exchanged becomes a central problem for our society, rather as in other societies (so anthropologists tell us) the regulation of systems of kinship was one of the basic elements in the regulation of social exchanges, solidarities and conflicts.

[2] *Urban Growth as a Theory of Communication* by H. Meier (M.I.T. Press).

III. To Re-establish Contact and get out of the Unequal Dialogue

A.—Re-establishing contact

In the perspective of the regulation of communications referred to above, it is very important to examine the origin of the breakdown in communication which has taken place. Often the breakdown is not primarily linked to psycho-sociological problems but, for instance, to disagreement on the plane of the images legitimizing the ideal functioning of social life. We have shown how much the idea of transparency could be a legitimizing image common to various tendencies. And yet it is at the origin of the breakdown on account of a misunderstanding—for this very image can be used to mean different things, so that it can legitimize very different aspects of collective life: one centred on harmony to be established here and now, the other centred on conflict as the condition of new creations. If we had time we could show how this gives rise to two totally different ways of perceiving the exercise of power and legitimate authority.

Faced with a difficulty of communication due to a breakdown of the cultural image, we cannot re-establish contact and make diversity into a condition of renewal unless a certain number of conditions are fulfilled. We shall try to throw light on these.

To begin with, none of the groups we are discussing should claim to have a monopoly of the truth. This presupposes the acceptance of initial disagreement and uncertainty concerning the subjects that will be progressively explored as they emerge from our encounters. Christians sometimes give this state of affairs biblical overtones: "Haven't we reached a time when we should all be aware that we can't separate the wheat from the tares; the Lord himself said he couldn't; if we did so there wouldn't be anything left in the fields." While others echo Amos with: "Who is righteous before God?"

If one of the groups cannot accept this attitude, for reasons it considers legitimate, then the breakdown of dialogue will go on, and it is not through avoiding broaching forbidden subjects that the problem will be resolved—that is to say subjects no one dares discuss for fear of splitting surface solidarities. On the contrary, as sometimes happens in the home, the area of these forbidden subjects risks becoming progressively larger and leading to a more and more superficial communication.

All this presupposes that we can develop possibilities of contact between diverse tendencies. But we should ask ourselves whether such contacts should be based on models of nineteenth-century political life, models on which our democracies are founded and where the juridical element is worked out in great detail. What we want to know is whether these juridical guarantees allow of an autonomy of expression of diverse tendencies. And here the organs of representation and public opinion come in. But how and what can public opinion mediate? Public opinion can, for instance, enable fringe currents of thought to be informed of the existence of other people reacting in the same way as themselves in other places, and this will enable them to become more rapidly aware of the "normality" of their reactions. In cases such as this, the speeding-up of the process by means of public opinion can make authority uneasy. In other cases public opinion can help authority to get out of a blind alley of communication by providing it with the public's reaction towards different problems. Thus it can mediate by causing dialogues to be started and by letting authority know the various existing reactions. Of course this brings with it certain disadvantages, but we may ask ourselves if a situation is healthy when authority has only individuals before it, individuals with a right to react in conscience eventually, but not a right to discuss with others with a view to forming groups from which they could explain their option and give it a certain publicity.

B. Setting up a more equal dialogue

Once we have discovered the origin of the breakdown and envisaged how to bring about a renewal of contact starting from the situation as it is, we can still hope to go further and make the dialogue less unequal. Now in this society centred on information, equality is closely linked with (among other things) a certain capacity for self-expression. It was in this connection that we recently heard of certain people in North America comparing one of the roles of the theologian with the role of the social animator in the urban environment. The social animator helps citizens at the bottom to express what they feel—for instance, about some aspect of town-planning that concerns them—and once their anxieties are better understood he helps them to formulate them in strong and suitably urbanized terms, thus enabling them to discuss, with parity of arms, with those responsible for the plan in question. Would it not be possible, these people suggested, for the theologian or priest to take on a similar role (this ambiguous language being due to the presence of lay theologians in the group). Thus the primary role of the theologian or the priest would not be to speak the truth in the group to which he belongs but, first and foremost, to help his group express what it feels and then to make these views explicit in correct theological language—thus, with parity of arms, initiating a discussion with others, including authority.

But the sociologist who questions himself as to this reaction will say that it implicitly presupposes a whole concept of the dynamics of the Church seen as a social group. The growth of the Church would then be closely linked with the places where the problem presents itself and with the groups which suffer most in their daily life from opposing demands and therefore feel themselves drawn, or even compelled, to express themselves. And this would certainly be a very important element in the building up of a less unequal dialogue. But to appreciate the importance of this element it must be seen as combined with the operation of mass communications which make it possible to circulate information about innovating movements independently of any control on the part of authority.

So there are two conditions for a more equal exchange contained here, and also, or so it seems to us, a way of analysing a re-establishment of exchanges for the growth of the group. One wonders, however, if this is a model adapted to what the Church wants to be. This question lies outside the framework of our analysis. Perhaps we could simply say that it is a model which, in the context of today, has a chance of being very catching, at least among innovating groups. However, social innovation is not created from within the silent majority . . . but that, too, is another problem.

Translated by Barbara Wall

Raymund Kottje

The Selection of Church Officials: Some Historical Facts and Experiences

AFTER the death of Cardinal Spellman, five hundred and sixty-three priests belonging to his archdiocese of New York sent a letter to the Pope at the beginning of 1968 asking to be allowed to participate in some way or other in the choice of Cardinal Spellman's successor. In the last three years similar petitions have frequently been made to the Pope when a bishopric fell vacant. Even where people did not turn to Rome—at Münster, for example, after the appointment of Bishop Höffner as co-adjutor to Cardinal Frings—there has often been very serious discussion of the question whether and how it was possible for clergy and people, that is, all the ordained and non-ordained Christians of a diocese, to share in the appointment of the new bishop. In isolated cases concrete steps have even been taken in this direction within the framework of the existing legal possibilities.

I. Discouraging Attitude of the Church Authorities

Up to now, in so far as Church authorities have adopted any attitude to these efforts, they have almost without exception declared themselves opposed to them. These authorities include first of all the Pope or the Roman Curia speaking through the papal nuncios, but also bishops and individual cathedral chapters. They based their opposition primarily on prevailing canon law. In fact, Canon 329 § 2 CIC does lay it down that bishops are appointed freely by the Pope, and even in Concordats containing clauses about the appointment of a new bishop there is in no case any provision for a body of electors larger than the cathedral chapter. In one instance (Speyer) attention was called to historical experience, and this was done simply to demonstrate what dangers arose for the Church out of earlier ways of appointing bishops.

However, the following glance at some phases in the history of the appointment of ecclesiastical dignitaries will show that the prevailing legal regulations are almost without exception the result of historical developments; that for this reason alone they cannot exclude the discussion of new possibilities; and that the one-sidedness with which solely negative experiences are cited from history is factually indefensible. I shall look mainly at the law as it existed, not so much at theories and principles of law, and for methodological and practical reasons I shall deal almost exclusively with the appointment of bishops, since this is central to the problem as a whole. Apart from this, only the selection of parish priests will be touched upon.

II. The Situation in Antiquity

The history of the appointment of Church dignitaries goes back to the New Testament. Alongside selection and appointment by individuals, either apostles or disciples of the apostles (Acts 14. 23; Tit. 1. 5), there is also talk in various different contexts of elections. It is sufficient here to recall the selection of Matthias by lot to replace Judas (Acts 1. 15 ff.) and the choice of the seven deacons (Acts 6. 2 ff.).

Even before the end of the first century the First Letter of Clement is speaking of officials appointed with the assent of the whole community (44. 3), and in the somewhat later Didache we find the instruction: "Choose yourselves bishops and deacons worthy of the Lord . . ." (15. 1).

How these elections were conducted we do not know. On the other hand, we have clear evidence from the third century that all members of the community had the right to vote, e.g., in the election of the bishop of Rome, although we are not entitled to equate this procedure with the universal suffrage of a modern democracy. This is evident from the distinction already to be found in Cyprian between the three elements in the appointment of a bishop: *populi suffragium, coepiscoporum consensus* and *divinum iudicium*. Thus the choice of the people had to be confirmed by the assent of the neighbouring bishops. The two elements together, choice and assent, expressed, so it was believed, the will of the Holy Spirit and thus God's decision in favour of the man chosen.

This is made still clearer by Ambrose, to whom we are indebted for an extremely illuminating account of the way in which bishops were chosen in his time. It occurs in his longest letter (Ep. 63), the one dating from the year 396 and addressed to the community of Vercelli. According to this, there were two parties to a canonical election: on one side the faithful of the city, and on the other the bishops of the province, whose presence at the ordination was regarded as indispensable. The people's contribution ranked as a plea or request; the decision lay with the bishops in consultation with the metropolitan. Either the bishops "ratified" the choice of the people or the latter agreed to the bishops' proposal. This corresponds with Pope Leo I's pronouncement dating from 458/59, that no one is to become a bishop unless he has been chosen by the clergy, requested by the people and, after the metropolitan has given his decision, consecrated by him and the other bishops of the province.

The importance of the people's part in the proceedings is shown not only by the well-known circumstances attending the election of Ambrose himself; it also becomes clear from the many internal disputes that preceded an election. In Rome in the year 366 they took an extremely bloody course; over a hundred people are said to have been killed.

In general it can be said that in the Western Church—and that is the only one with which we are concerned here—it was taken for granted that the local communities should participate in the appointment of deacons, presbyters and bishops, whether through direct election, assent (acclamation) or bearing witness. In addition, in the choice of bishops, there was the participation of the neighbouring bishops and the confirmation of the choice by the metropolitan enjoined by the Council of Nicaea in 325 as an expression of the Church's consciousness of unity.

However, the collaboration of clergy and people was not seen as the sovereign right, so to speak, of Christian communities;

rather was it understood in the sense that the community was acting as a society of those endowed in baptism with the spirit of God and inspired now by this same Holy Spirit. To this extent, the choice of dignitaries was always regarded as assent to the will of God and as the outcome of the activity of the Holy Spirit. General agreement on the choice, to which the greatest importance was attached, though it by no means implied unanimity, was seen as a sign of the divine decision in favour of the new dignitary.

III. The Choice of Dignitaries in the Middle Ages

Of course, the firmer the legal basis given to the hierarchical organization of the Church—and this means from the fourth century onwards in particular—the stronger became the effort in many places to force the community into a passive role. Moreover, in many dioceses the number of people in the community was increasing considerably, so that precisely in the big, important communities choice by the people as a whole was becoming in practice illusory. None the less, the people retained a share in the appointment of bishops well on into the Middle Ages. The old ecclesiastical principle, "He whom all should obey must also be chosen by all", was accepted far and wide, at any rate in theory. In the context of our inquiry it is of only secondary importance that electoral rights and methods differed individually from place to place, sometimes even from one election to the next in the same place.

To be sure, the often formal-sounding references to the participation of clergy and people cannot hide the fact that in practice it had long been almost everywhere only a small circle that could exert a decisive effect on the appointment of a bishop. This circle comprised mainly men who were influential because of their ecclesiastical, political or social position, primarily members of the nobility, but also probably the heads of respected monasteries and foundations, abbots and deans.

In the Germanic lands the attitude of the king was in many cases from the early Middle Ages onward even more decisive. This is understandable when one thinks of the political importance of bishops since the days of Constantine. Moreover, in the

Germanic countries their importance had for various reasons considerably increased; it had grown particularly great in the East Frankish kingdom since the middle of the tenth century, when Otto I had given the bishops royal authority. The king was now bound to have an even greater interest than before in seeing that only a man whom he trusted acquired a vacant bishopric. The mass of clergy and people, on the other hand, was confined more and more to a ritual participation. This did not mean, according to the view prevailing in those days, that they were excluded from the election. "The wish of the king was certainly the deciding factor, but the form in which it achieved fulfilment was the *electio* by the clergy and people. Without this a canonical appointment could not be made" (Schmid 23). It was not a free election in the sense of a completely free decision, but it did express the people's right to have a say in the appointment of a bishop and not to be compelled to accept any official against their will.

A new development in the history of the law and practice of filling bishoprics occurred in the second half of the eleventh century. The reforming forces which gained a wide influence on ecclesiastical life at that time, especially under Gregory VII (1073–85) and his successors, reacted sharply against the fact that the selection and enthronement (investiture) of bishops had become largely the prerogative of the king or high-ranking nobles, that is, of lay powers, and were conducted primarily in accordance with political considerations. The reformers emphasized the ecclesiastical and spiritual character of the business of filling bishoprics and demanded a return to the old ways of choosing bishops, that is, ways involving a decisive contribution from clergy and people. At the same time they also claimed for the Pope the right to have the elections supervised and checked by his legates, and, in the case of disputed elections, to take on himself the final decision about the appointment. Thus in demanding the restoration of the election Gregory was fighting not only for the communities and their freedom of choice, but also for the papacy. Wherever he made a demand for the restoration of the election he was also concerned—explicitly or implicitly—with making good the claim that the elections were subject to the control of the papal legates.

In parallel with this development there was a tendency, which grew more and more decided, to confine the right to a vote, not only in practice but also in law, to a smaller circle of electors, and a clerical one at that. In the course of the twelfth century the participation of the people slipped more and more into the background. Almost everywhere the choice was made predominantly by the diocesan clergy, and from the end of the century onwards by the cathedral chapter alone. It is true that numerous disputes, often provoked not by conflicts within the Church but by political motives on a national or family level, show how strongly selection continued to be influenced by political powers. In spite of this, the result of developments in the century after Gregory VII was undoubtedly a clear clericalization of the electoral body and the assumption by the Pope of an influence on the filling of bishoprics which on the whole he had never had before.

This influence increased considerably in connection with the development of the Pope's monarchical power from the time of Alexander III (1159–1181) onwards and with the growth of late medieval papalism and curialism. By way of a number of very different canonical grounds for intervention, the Popes claimed and acquired wider and wider rights in the appointment of bishops. And from rights in individual cases—by further development of the legal norms put forward in these cases—was deduced the Pope's general right to appoint all bishops by virtue of the supreme pastoral authority vested in him. As a result, by the end of the Middle Ages, the electoral rights of bodies such as cathedral chapters were often regarded, in accordance with this conception, as, from a legal point of view, privileges granted by the Pope. It must not be overlooked that not the least of the driving forces behind this development were the political and financial interests of the Popes and the Curia.

IV. The Selection of Parish Priests

It was also mainly financial interests which led in the same period to a successful expansion of the papal rights in the granting of lower ecclesiastical offices (e.g., canonries, parishes and curacies). Nevertheless, in this sphere community voting rights were in many places retained or freshly acquired, especially in the appointment of custodians of church property, of parish priests and of assistant priests. Even in the choice of parish priests, it is true, communities were not on the whole entrusted with the task of actually selecting the candidates, but again simply with that of giving their consent to the proposal put forward by a committee of clerics—e.g., in bigger communities the other parish clergy or the clergy of a deanery chapter. However, the possibility of collaborating in the appointment of the parish priest was granted mainly to the populations of towns. In rural parishes the appointment was very often a right belonging to lords of particular churches, to monasteries and foundations; after the twelfth century, where the parishioners had the right to be consulted the parishes concerned were for the most part fairly new ones.

V. The Situation in Modern Times

In spite of the clericalization of those electoral bodies still extant and in spite of the ever more unrestricted bestowal of high and even lowly Church offices by the Pope, political powers— kings, landowners, and even cities—nevertheless retained influence over ecclesiastical appointments right into modern times or even acquired it for the first time. It fell to them by right, or sometimes purely as a result of the balance of power. Where they did not or could not disregard electoral rights, they very often managed to influence electoral bodies in accordance with their own interests. Even though this influence was frequently exerted only in the interests of pure power politics, it must not be overlooked that many princes and cities were concerned to select capable and worthy candidates for ecclesiastical office. For the rest, it is only too easy to understand that, in view of the political importance of both the higher and the lower clergy, people had a vital interest in seeing that Church posts were filled by loyal men.

This interest is not the least important of the reasons why in the nineteenth- and twentieth-century Concordats with European states there are clauses giving the respective governments rights of various different kinds in the appointment of bishops. The crucial point in these clauses is the one concerned with the government's ability to exclude a candidate not acceptable to it; in general, the way in which the preceding choice of candidates is to be made is of secondary importance, even if this procedure is laid down in the Concordat.

VI. PARALLELS BETWEEN THE CHURCH AND SOCIETY

However, the history of the selection of bishops, which I have outlined very briefly here, with a quick glance at the selection of parish priests, can only be properly understood and evaluated if we see that it did not run its course in isolation from political and social life. For it can be observed that the changes in the participation of clergy and people in the appointment of bishops have a remarkable parallel in the changing share of the people in political life, especially at the local level.

In the territory of the late Roman Empire the similarities between ecclesiastical and political elections are so clear—they extend even to the verbal formulas used—that they justify the assumption that in the moulding of their style of life the Christians of the first few centuries utilized their experience of their own political environment and, among other things, took over the forms of election usual in those days.

There is also a parallel in the development of the electoral body. In Roman towns, from the fifth century onwards, it was only an upper stratum that had any decisive say in the choice of important town officials, as in the choice of bishops. It is therefore not incorrect to assert that ecclesiastical elections in late antiquity cannot be understood without a glance at the prevailing constitutional arrangements and social order.

Another equally significant example which should be adduced to illustrate the parallel between ecclesiastical and politico-social development is offered by the medieval city-states of northern Italy from the second half of the eleventh century onwards. Here, in the context of local self-government, communities displayed a strengthened desire to participate in decisions, and one of the ways in which this desire found expression was in the effort to acquire a stronger influence on the appointment of ecclesiastical dignitaries. In central and western Europe, too, the striving in the towns for a share in the choice of parish priests is bound up everywhere with the urge for freedom, i.e., for self-determination, an urge that had been increasing since the twelfth century and was connected with the older idea of partnership. On the other hand, the course of development which in the last six to seven centuries has swept aside almost completely electoral rights in the Church has unmistakable parallels in the development of the forms of rule which predominated in Europe for centuries. It is only the transition to democratic modes of political life, now a reality far and wide, that has so far not been accomplished in the ecclesiastical field—apart from a few beginnings.

VII. Prospect

However, such beginnings are so far not apparent in the appointment of Church officials and hence in the choice and appointment of bishops. Yet might it not be to the advantage of the Church that people accustomed to elect their political representatives, either directly or indirectly, should also acquire some influence on the appointment of their ecclesiastical supervisors? On the other hand, we must also ask very seriously whether the Church should or dare adopt without examining them the political forms of the prevailing society, i.e., in this context, the methods of appointing dignitaries. Instead of considering this question in the abstract, let us look beyond the historical evidence previously adduced, at the experience of the Evangelical Church in Germany.

When, after 1918, this Church had to proceed on its own responsibility to reorganize its constitution, ecclesiastical suffrage was modelled on that of the state, and thus democratized. In the time of the Weimar Republic church elections went off without any friction. But the dangers bound up with the new voting rights became apparent at once in the elections of 1933. Under party political pressure, egged on by a speech of Hitler's, Evangelical Christians voted in greater numbers than ever before and the majority of them voted for the list of "German Christians" devoted to the National Socialist regime. As a result, the representatives of these "German Christians" were able to occupy, perfectly legally, central positions in the Evangelical Church.

The danger encountered in 1933 by the Evangelical Church, that in elections for Church dignitaries political or other alien interests can exert a decisive influence, is fundamentally not new, as our survey of some phases in the history of the choice of bishops in particular may have shown. This danger still exists today and will continue to do so in the future. It is not completely eliminated even by the Pope's present almost unlimited rights in the filling of bishops' thrones.

On the other hand, as history also shows, this papal right is not the outcome of one particular course of development or even of one determined mainly by ecclesiastical thinking. It would therefore be thoroughly appropriate for the Church, as an historical power, to look for new ways of appointing ecclesiastical dignitaries. In such an undertaking it would be necessary to take into account both tradition—the whole tradition, not just that of the last seven centuries—and the present structure of political and social life.[1]

[1] There is an extensive literature on the subject of this article. Of the older works, it will suffice to mention P. Schmid's still fundamental work, *Der Begriff der kanonischen Wahl in den Anfängen des Investiturstreits* (Stuttgart, 1926). The following references are confined to a few more recent publications: H. E. Feine, *Kirchliche Rechtsgeschichte*, Bd. I; *Die Katholische Kirche* (Cologne, 1964), esp. pp. 118, 342 f., 380/2; D. Kurze, "Pfarrerwahlen im Mittelalter", *Forschungen zur kirchlichen Rechtsgeschichte und zum Kirchenrecht* 6 (Cologne, 1966); R. L. Benson, *The Bishop-Elect*: A Study in Medieval Ecclesiastical Office (Princeton, N.J., 1968); P. G. Caron, "Les élections épiscopales dans la doctrine et la pratique de l'Eglise", *Cahiers de Civilisation Médiévale* 11 (1968), pp. 579–85; G. Hoffmann, "Wahlen und Ämterbesetzung in der Kirche, *Festschrift für E. Ruppel* 4 (Hannover, 1968), pp. 164–96 (mainly discusses problems of the Evangelical Church in Germany); G. Biemer, "Die Bischofswahl als neues Desiderat kirchlicher Praxis", *Theol. Quartalschr*, 149 (1969), pp. 171–84; H. Schmitz, "Plädoyer für Bischofs- und Pfarrerwahl", *Trierer Theol. Zeitschr*. 79 (1970), pp. 230–49.

Translated by J. R. Foster

Peter Huizing

The Problem of the Division of Governmental Functions in the Church

THE old three-sided doctrine according to which three arms of authority—the legislative to draw up universally binding rules, the executive to apply them, and the judicial to test the application against the rules—are ascribable to three reciprocally independent organs was long ago shown to be a gross simplification. Of course we distinguish, in fairly general terms, three fundamental duties of government—legislation, administration and the execution of justice—to be distributed among, or assigned to, various organs in such a way that with a proper balance being maintained between them they can be carried out as effectively as may be. An ideal model for this distribution—one suitable for every time and place—does not exist. Of course, we can set out appropriate principles. Thus for a constitutional state one fundamental principle is that of legitimacy, the requirement that duties and competencies and norms for the functioning of governmental organs be clearly defined; that everyone enjoy adequate legal protection against wrongful, illegal acts on the part of government; that jurisdiction in such cases be exercised by bodies independent of other governmental organs; that in the assignment of functions to this or that higher or lower organ due attention be paid to the principle of subordination, and so forth.

On 7 October 1967 the Episcopal Synod approved a number of principles for the revision of the Ecclesiastical Code. No. 7 states that accepting the principle of judicial protection against unlawful governmental action, the various functions of authority in the Church—the legislative, administrative and judicial functions—must be distinguished and the organs which exercise them defined.

I. Separation of Legislative and Administrative Organs?

Legislating for the *universal Church* and for the Latin patriarchate is the preserve of the Pope and an ecumenical council. The Congregations of the College of Cardinals are often described as executive organs. With the introduction of the Ecclesiastical Code it was laid down that they are to issue no universally binding regulations—except in the case of extreme necessity—but give effect to the laws by means of instructions and the like. They have nevertheless issued a large number of universally binding regulations, albeit with the Pope's approval. What is more, from 1918 on they had the biggest share in papal legislation. Their function did not and could not remain restricted to putting into effect papal laws which had come into being without their knowledge or consent. Initiative power, preparatory organizing, the framing of legislative proposals, exerting an opinion-forming influence upon the Pope—all this has emanated very largely from the curia. Juridically speaking—and in a theoretical or formal sense—the Pope was the sole law-maker; in practice legislation resulted from collaboration between Pope and curia. The juridical structure guarantees that the curia is never entitled to claim ascendancy over the Pope; it does not guarantee that the Pope will in fact have a more decisive part in its determinations than the curia or certain members or coteries within it.

With the inauguration of the *Synod of Bishops* on 15 September 1965 a new factor was brought into play. It is an agency of the world-wide episcopate; but the heads of the Roman dicasteries also sit as members of it. It is to be hoped that the broad features of papal policy and legislation for the Church will come to be more powerfully influenced by the Synod than by the curia, without loss to the latter of its administrative and in a broad sense legislative function. The setting up of a council of bishops by the general secretariat of the Synod on 23 March 1970 has served to strengthen its position.

Within the *diocese* the only authority having legislative powers in a strictly legal sense is the bishop. The advisory function of the diocesan synod has turned out in practice to be inefficient and has everywhere been allowed to lapse. As appears from a document put out by the Congregation for the Clergy, and dated 11 April 1970, the intention now is to make the priests' council the bishop's main advisory body. The title and function of "the bishop's senate for the management of the diocese" have been reserved for this. Specifically mentioned as one of its duties is the task of advising on diocesan statutes proposed for possible ratification; but all matters of importance are supposed to be dealt with in the council. The provincial council is the officially legislative organ within the province, the bishops' conference in matters specified by the law for its area; here again it is the bishops alone whose voice is decisive.

The legislative function is a relatively modest part, after all, of the governmental responsibilities of *Pope and bishops*. They are more administrators than legislators. For both functions they have at their disposal the same advisory and executive organs. Neither the Roman curia nor the bishops have ever yet demonstrated the need to change this and to create different organs for performing these functions. A few theoreticians are in favour of that, without having shown us what the advantages would be. Most have argued for reserving official legislative and administrative competency not to the Pope alone and the bishop alone but to the Episcopal Synod with the Pope, and to the priests' council or pastoral council with the bishop.

What is much more important, urgent and imperative is that during the stages *before* any officially legal decision is taken— the period of initiatory action, of consultation, of opinion-forming and decision-making—Pope and bishops have access to, and are personally in free and open contact with, organs that are representative of the *whole* Church: not only of bishops and clergy; not only of old people and middle-aged people; not only of conservatives and middle-of-the-road groups; not only of theologians and canonists. The great trouble with the much needed democracy in the process of administration and law-making in the Roman curia and in most episcopal curias too is the absence of an opposition, of any representation of the Left, of criticism coming from independent laymen and especially from young people. All this has a paralysing and frustrating effect on the present-day community's appraisal of the ruling authority's policies. It is not remedied by clerics taking a collegial line among themselves or by separating out legislative organs from administrative ones. What would help is assigning to all sections and schools of thought the right to active participation in opinion- and decision-forming processes at all levels of church government.

II. Administrative Jurisdiction

Administrative jurisdiction is jurisdiction in respect of differences or disputes to which the governing authority is itself a party. Such differences may exist between governmental organs, for instance, over the demarcation of competencies; or between governmental organs and private parties who believe that the governing authority has infringed their rights. Until a short time ago this last kind of administrative jurisdiction had no place in church order. Canon 1667 of the Ecclesiastical Code does of course specify that every right can be vindicated by an action before the court, unless different provision is made; but canon 1601 had already made such exceptional provision in stipulating that against supreme ordinaries no appeal to the Rota is possible, but that in respect of such appeals judgment is to be given exclusively by the Roman Congregations. In other words, one cannot embark upon an action before an ecclesiastical court against wrongful acts committed by the church authorities; one can only address oneself to a higher ecclesiastical authority. Church courts have even declined to handle disputes about matters which in one way or another had engaged the attention of a Roman Congregation.

For several decades past canonists of repute have been contending for the importation of administrative jurisdiction into church order. Objections levelled against the Roman procedure have been weighty enough: distances and differences of language have made it difficult to ascertain and reach a judgment upon facts, have slowed down the proceedings, have given rise to misunderstandings; hearings in camera and decisions arrived at without any reasons for them being given have failed to satisfy a sense of justice; obscure and unstable jurisprudence has resulted in *legal insecurity*. One could assume that the curia was going about its work with due care and warranty; one would have liked to see that clearly demonstrated to boot. The self-reliance and responsibility of the faithful *vis-à-vis* the authorities, reinforced by Vatican II, has increased the likelihood of conflicts arising and also the need for a clear judicial procedure and dispensing of justice.

A first step in the right direction was taken with the Constitution *Regimini ecclesiae universae*, of 15 August 1967, on the reform of the Roman curia. Article no. 106 of that document assigns to the second section of the Apostolic Signature the task of adjudicating on disputes arising from an act on the part of ecclesiastical authority and referred to the Signature on appeal against a decision taken by a competent dicastery whenever it is presumed that the said act has abrogated a law. In these cases the Signature determines either the acceptance of the appeal or the legality of the disputed act.

A person who believes that his rights have been infringed by an administrative act, for instance, on the part of his bishop, must therefore *first* turn to the *Congregation empowered* to deal with the question; and only then has he the right to *appeal to the Signature* against the Congregation's verdict. Some writers consider that if the conflict results from an action taken by the Congregation itself—for example, if a bishop thinks it has acted unlawfully towards him—no appeal to the Signature is possible. Neither from the wording of no. 106 of the Constitution *Regimini* nor from the nature of the case is it evident why any distinction should be made between a wrongful decision in a previous (preliminary) dispute and a wrongful decision without that circumstance; nor is any sign of such a distinction apparent from the special norms of the Signature of 25 March 1968. Article 96 (1) lays it down that through the second section the Signature is to take cognizance of disputes arising from an action on the part of ecclesiastical authority, taken before it on appeal against a decision made by a competent dicastery, every time a breach of the law is alleged.

Administrative jurisdiction does not pronounce as to the expediency of this or that administrative action, but only as to its legality. Some commentators are inclined to narrow down the concept of "right" by confining "illegality" to infringement of a positive church law, and of that alone. I reckon this restriction

to be at odds with the purpose and object of administrative jurisdiction, which is to give full protection against unlawful acts on
the part of the governing authority—and moreover at odds with
the nature of church law in general, where the force of "natural
law" and "divine law" is recognized to be primary. The governing authority behaves unlawfully not only when it fails to maintain a positive law, but also if and when it infringes the basic
rights of a human being and of a Christian or acts contrary to
universally valid principles of decent government. Abuse of
power, disparate handling of similar cases, unreasoned or unexplained decisions, depriving people of their legal security, a
kind of indifference to the community—these are so many examples of unlawfulness, "unrightfulness", against which there
must be protection in law.

In pursuance of the above-mentioned principles for the revision of the Ecclesiastical Code the new law is bound to go considerably further. No. 6, on the protection of the rights of the
person, states that authority in the Church is vested in Pope and
bishops, but that the use of that authority cannot be arbitrary, and
the rights of each and every church member must be acknowledged and protected. No. 7, on the protection of subjective
rights, states that in canon law the principle of legal protection
must be applied equally to those in command and those under
them, so as to put a stop completely to any suspicion of arbitrary
conduct in the government of the Church. On the question of
appeal the law must so provide that if anyone considers his rights
to have been infringed by a lower authority, this can be effectively
redressed by a higher one.

It is the general view among canonists that in ecclesiastical
practice and the dispensing of justice administrative appeals fall
short of the mark. Everywhere there is felt to be a need for instituting *various grades and types of administrative tribunal*, so
that there the maintenance of justice would have its own canonical procedure, which competent bodies of this or that different
grade would follow. The Code will have to define what actions
can be entered into with the administrative tribunals, work out
the norms for the administrative process, create stable organs for
this dispensation of justice. It is simpler to organize administrative jurisdiction as it concerns the acts of a directing authority,

but not so simple when appeal has to be allowed against legislation on the part of lower authorities in so far as that conflicts with legislation by higher ones. One would wish every legal proceeding to be in public, except if there are certain cases in which the judge directs otherwise. Anyone who has lodged an appeal— or indeed the respondent—must be informed about everything that is being adduced against him.

In accordance with these principles the new law will have to include a comprehensive system of administrative tribunals or courts of justice.

III. MEDIATION AND ARBITRATION

The *Canon Law Society of America*, at its 31st annual conference, 20–23 October 1969, received *nem. con.* a report that concerned itself chiefly with methods of preventing or resolving conflicts in the Church. The best solution of all is by means of conciliation to bring the parties to a conflict together and to help them settle their differences. The conciliator gives no ruling. A *diocese* should be able to set up a *"conciliation board"* to which anybody could turn who has a dispute with any other person or body within the diocese. Canons 1925 *et seq.* of the Ecclesiastical Code provide a point of departure for this, in that the judge is recommended to try to bring the parties to a friendly settlement and persuade them not to proceed with the action. With this sort of mediation the aim is more to reconcile people who are in conflict than to determine rights and obligations on this side and on that. In a church community, therefore, this must be the primary way of resolving conflicts.

Canons 1929 *et seq.* lay it down that in order to avoid a judicial process the parties may also agree to have a ruling on the dispute between them given by one or more arbiters of their choice. *A propos* of that the report suggests that in each diocese or in several dioceses together an *office of arbitration* be set up, with the job of assisting parties to come to arbitration. In pursuance of agreement parties are bound to submit to the judgment of the arbiter(s). They may themselves determine whether the arbitrating body must find in accordance with strict justice or with equity (fair compromise). It is desirable that appeal from this decision should still be possible in the event that the rules of the agreement or of arbitration have not been correctly upheld. For both procedures—conciliation and arbitration—the report provides examples in the form of detailed models.

Conciliation and arbitration offer a solution in individual cases; they do not shape law. In addition, there must be development in the sphere of administrative jurisdiction. Interpretation of the law by the judge, a from case to case more precise definition of rights by the judge, legal precedent, especially for the assessment and protection of the rights of Christians—these are fundamental values where church government is concerned. For so long as a new system of administrative courts of justice has not yet begun to operate, the bishops could delegate judicial powers either to existing diocesan courts or to boards or tribunals especially charged with giving judgment on disputes arising out of acts of one kind or another performed by the governing authority. Experiments in this field could be of value to the commission charged with the revision of this part of canon law.

Literature

We, the People of God . . . A Study of Constitutional Government for the Church, ed. James A. Coriden (1968).

Canon Law Society of America. Proceedings of the Thirty-First Annual Convention (Cleveland, Ohio, 20–23 October 1969).

Ign. Gordon, "De Tribunalibus administrativis propositis a Commissione Codici Iuris Canonici recognoscendo et suffragatis ab Episcoporum Synodo", in *Periodica de re morali canonica liturgica* 57 (1968), pp. 602–52; *id.*, "Normae speciales Supremi Tribunalis Signaturae Apostolicae", *ib.* 59 (1970), pp. 75–165.

H. Schmitz, "Möglichkeit und Gestalt einer kirchlichen Gerichtsbarkeit über die Verwaltung", in *Archiv für katholisches Kirchenrecht* 135 (1966), pp. 18–38; "Pontificia Commissio Codici Iuris Canonici recognoscendo". *Communicationes*, 2 December 1969.

Translated by Hubert Hoskins

Jan Kerkhofs

The Dutch Pastoral Council as a Model for a Democratic Church Assembly

IN his letter of 24 December 1969 to Cardinal Alfrink and the Dutch bishops on the eve of the fifth plenary meeting of the Pastoral Council Paul VI expressed the grave reservations he felt regarding the points of doctrine contained in the draft reports (on priesthood and religious life). He went on: "Reservations of a different character—but, it would appear, equally well grounded —have been advanced in the press, relating to the test applied to ensure a proper representation of Dutch Catholics in this plenary meeting."[1]

I. A COMPLEX SITUATION

The Dutch bishops in their statement of 19 January 1970 issued to the press alluded to the problems of representation and of the relation of the churches to one another within the universal Church. Having established that "the fifth plenary session has made it clear what ideas about the tie-up between celibacy and priesthood are current among a considerable section of Dutch church people", the bishops admit to realizing "that another section of the church community holds to a different opinion". This creates a complex situation. "The same diversity of view exists in other parts of the Church as well. One section of Dutch church people—however large a proportion it may be—cannot and must not insist that its outlook be shared without further discussion by the Church as a whole." The bishops are ascertaining

[1] Katholiek Archief, 25 (1970), pp. 77-9.

135

the repercussions of one province in other parts of the Church, for instance, through the publicity media. They confirm that they "bear responsibility for their own part of the Church, but at the same time carry responsibility for the Church universal".

Thus there came about a very strained situation: on the one hand the representative character of the Dutch Pastoral Council is called in question, on the other what is being called in doubt (by implication) is the representative nature of the papal pronouncement for the world Church. The key questions, however, are being avoided: namely, whether the Pastoral Council really did make unrepresentative statements; whether, if the reverse is true, the bishops are bound to fall in with it; whether the opinion of Paul VI, of the Curia, and of the sees in agreement with them is representative and, if not, whether these last are obliged to seek after what will genuinely represent ideas within the Church and so endorse them on all points or in this or that particular.

However, the problems go deeper than that: to what extent can the "public opinion" of the people of God be regarded as an expression of the *sensus Ecclesiae* and of the original Tradition?[2] To what extent is this public opinion among the faithful measurable (in which case one should allow for all the complexity of the relation of *élite* to masses with respect to evaluative behaviour and experience)? The next thing will be for the sociologist to start asking about the orientation and content of "public opinion" within the ecclesiastical hierarchy as a subgroup,[3] whether of the episcopal curias or of the Vatican, and about the tension there may be between this "public opinion" and that of the people of God. Hooking on to this, the theologian may then put his question as to the criteria for distinguishing the operation of the Spirit: whether the Spirit, in a given period or conjuncture, is to be found more obviously among the leaders as a group than among the people. Having regard to the very widespread "credibility crisis" in the contemporary Church, it would look as

[2] Y. Congar, *La Tradition et les traditions* (Paris, 1960); K. Rahner, "Öffentliche Meinung in der Kirche", in *Orientierung* (1951), p. 255; K. Rahner, "Glaubenskongregation und Theologenkommission heute", in *Stimmen der Zeit*, 95 (April, 1970), pp. 225-7.
[3] Cf., e.g., in a context of the sociology of knowledge, the encyclical *Quod Apostolici Muneris* (28 Dec. 1878) of Pope Leo XIII with his encyclical *Rerum Novarum* (15 May 1891).

though questions of this sort are not to be dismissed out of hand.[4]

It is impossible to shed light on every aspect of this problem here. We would simply like to state the question of representivity at two levels: that is, is the Pastoral Council representative; and are the results of the January 1970 ballot representative?

II. The Query regarding the Degree and Quality of Representation

While the Dutch bishops were still in Rome, they announced in a pastoral letter of 8 December 1965 that Vatican II would be implemented in The Netherlands by means of a "provincial Council". Originally, when thought was given to this Council, it was still very much in juridical categories; but the *"jus conditum"* was soon dropped in favour of the *"jus condendum"*: post-conciliar theology and the conditions prevailing in a modern society like the Dutch call for new forms of management and consultation in the Church. That is why preference was given to the term "Pastoral Council". It is in this sense that the term "pastoral Council" is to be understood. The point was, in fact, to involve the whole body of the faithful, with their needs and desires and wants, in these deliberations of a local Church within the universal Church. Moreover, any real discussion within a Dutch context entailed from the very start co-operation on the part of the other Churches and of the humanist connection.

During his press conference held on 14 November 1966 Cardinal Alfrink said: "Our Pastoral Council is a free, open communication in faith and love, which means we would be happy indeed if barriers could be broken down and if it were to be possible for unity and unanimity to increase. It is meant to be a fully shared pastoral council where each and every voice may be heard and any idea may be given an airing. . . . It is very important that in this pastoral council we take the church community of the Dutch province seriously as being a fellowship of all believers

[4] Klaus Hemmerle, "Zur Theologie der Repräsentativität in der Kirche" (es geht um die Darstellung Christi), in *Rheinischer Merkur* (17 April 1970); H. Hoefnagels, *Demokratisierung der kirchlichen Autorität* (Vienna, 1969).

and that we ensure that all are involved and have their say. That is communication; and to that end channels enabling it to flow are being forged in a period of reconstruction which commands respect for all who have already turned their attention to it."

Thus in 1967, in all the dioceses taken together, there were a good 15,000 discussion groups sponsored by the Council, the activities of which were relayed in diocesan reports to the Council itself.[5] Furthermore, it was made possible for anyone to communicate via special P.O. boxes with the Council (these letters were all dealt with by a team of pastoral correspondents). Out of the experiences culled during the period between the end of 1965 and the middle of 1967 there emerged a working formula accepted as an obligatory element for the further operation of the Council. On 18 July 1967 it received the approval of the Dutch episcopate.[6]

The circulatory or channelling system which it embodies is here summarized. The task of the Council assembled in plenary session is: "(1) to give a decision on the question of whether the correspondence dealt with reflects the faithful thinking of the church community; (2) to settle whether it is desirable that certain practical conclusions be attached to the ideas and insights expressed". This assembly comprises at the most 150 members, including: the bishops and assistant bishops; the central committee, the representatives chosen by (but not necessarily from) the diocesan pastoral councils (from each diocese 3 priests, secular or regular, and 7 lay people); 10 religious, chosen from and by the male and female religious orders; a maximum of 15 persons nominated by the bishops (to ensure that a proper balance is preserved in the group as a whole). Invited as members without vote are: delegates from other Churches, religious communities and groups representing this or that outlook on life.

III. The Structure

The bishops constitute the praesidium of the plenary assembly. Together with the central committee they fix the agenda. At the

---

[5] It became clear from the first meetings of the advisers that young people were under-represented.

[6] *Ratio vel formula agendi in celebrando Concilio Pastorali* (Rotterdam, 1967).

beginning of a session the plenary assembly may, of course, with an absolute majority of votes and within the limits of its competency, decide to add items to this agenda. If the plenary assembly declares itself by means of a vote regarding matters laid before it, a two-thirds majority of the voting members present is required (the bishops, as official leaders in the faith, cast their vote first).

Besides the plenary assembly the Council has two organs: the central committee (with a maximum of 7 members, appointed by the bishops), which is charged with the immediate preparatory work, and a consultative board. This board is composed of 8 specialists or qualified experts, a representative of the work-group concerned with the "conciliar discussion groups", a representative of the "post-boxes" work-group and one from the other Churches. Care was taken to employ a system of selection that would result in a body at once fairly representative and expert.

Furthermore, steps have been taken to ensure that although it must of course be incomplete, there will be as much debate and consultation as possible worked into the process of shaping the documents. In summary form it amounts to this: the praesidium draws up the items for the agenda; the consultative board arranges for this material to be studied by some 15 (later 16) study-committees; the reports of these committees go to the board, are sent back to the committees if necessary, and then via the board find their way to the central committee; these reports are then passed—if necessary, as confidential matter—to the diocesan pastoral councils for discussion and comment. Only then do the reports come before the plenary assembly.

In the memorandum designed to comment on and explain this procedure reference is made in some detail to the distinctive and irreducible authority and the responsibility of the bishops.[7] Whereas at first the idea had been to set up an advisory Council of experts whose job would be to prepare reports on the basis of which the bishops could take decisions, this model was very quickly dropped in favour of that of a joint council of bishops,

[7] Cardinal Alfrink defined very clearly the proper function of the Bishops in his opening address at the fourth plenary assembly. See *Past. Concilie van de Nederlandse Kerkprovincie*, pt. 5 (Katholiek Archief, 1969), pp. 201–2.

priests, religious and people. Thus the bishops stand at one and the same time within and over against the plenary assembly. This latter is required to pronounce on the question whether the reports reflect the thinking, in good faith, of the church community and what concrete consequences, if any, that might entail. In all quarters the aim has been much more to reach, through dialogue, a general agreement as to the stances to be adopted than to discuss the reports in detail or to vote on this or that particular pastoral recommendation.

Of course one can raise the question: are the 15,000 discussion groups, the incoming letters, the members chosen by the diocesan pastoral councils and by the religious orders entirely representative? To this the answer is bound to be "no": a lot of people have refused to participate—and for the most diverse reasons, such as lack of interest, individualism, silent, implicit protest. How are we to know whether we are here dealing with a "silent minority" or a "silent majority"? But does not this defect, this weakness, of the democratic rules of procedure operate all over the place— in parliaments, local councils, trade unions, universities and cultural organizations? And is it not the normal thing for those who are most heavily engaged to determine the way things will go?

IV. The Fifth Plenary Assembly

It was in connection with the fifth plenary assembly that the question of the degree and quality of representation was raised in the sharpest terms, for instance, in a statement made by the Vatican chief-of-press, Mgr Fausto Vallainc, and in declarations on the part of a number of Dutch Catholic groups. J. Bluyssen, the bishop of 's Hertogenbosch, replied to these questionings in a pastoral letter as follows:[8]

(a) At the Pastoral Council as well as in their declaration of 19 January the bishops expressly stated that a substantial group thinks differently with regard to celibacy; the bishops are extremely well aware of this!

(b) Thus the Pastoral Council of January last year, in the

---

[8] Pastoral letter of 27 February 1970; see *Archief der Kerken*, 25 (1970), pp. 257-8.

opinion it expressed on the obligatory celibacy of priests, was much more unanimous than are Dutch Catholics as a whole; as people may find it surprising, or something of a scandal, it is better to involve all the evidence, including that from outside the Council, in one's judgment; and that the bishops did, when they formulated their policy in this matter.

(c) On the basis of various soundings of opinion during recent years—soundings which invariably yield more or less the same percentage—one is entitled to assume that about 70% of our Catholic people, in one way or another, want to see a change in the law of celibacy; it is difficult, therefore, to accept—what one can still hear being asserted—that the great majority will have none of it.

The statements regarding a married priesthood agreed by the plenary assembly at all events reflect, albeit in a somewhat more pronounced form, all inquiries on the subject that have been carried out in the Netherlands, those conducted explicitly among priests as well as those conducted among the people. On any ordinary view, therefore, one has to conclude that even if the composition of the plenary assembly is insufficiently democratic, the majority of the faithful do in fact concur with the resolutions of that assembly.[9] Cardinal Alfrink, in his opening address at the fourth plenary session (7 April 1969), justly pointed out that the Dutch attempt to democratize the Church could not from the very start be a complete success, although it is to be hoped that in the Church the running-in period will not have to last for centuries, as was the case with democracy in the political sphere.

The democratic method of the Dutch Pastoral Council is certainly imperfect: young people, women, parish priests, for instance, have not been sufficiently involved with the Council. The

[9] "Zo denkt Katholiek Nederland", E. W.-Nipo inquiry, *Elseviers-weekblad* 25 (1969), pp. 75–83.
—*Het Priestercelibaat*; Intomart-investigation on behalf of the K.R.O. (1970).
—*Hoe denken de gelovigen over de celibaatswet?* Results of investigation. Series: *De Kerk van Morgen* (Amersfoort) (Rotterdam, 1968); *Priestercelibaat. Een probleem van de Kerk.* Series: *Kerk van Morgen* (Amersfoort) (Rotterdam, 1969).
—*Ambtscelibaat in een veranderende Kerk.* Results of an inquiry among all priests, deacons and subdeacons in the Netherlands. Series: *Kerk van Morgen* (Amersfoort) (Rotterdam, 1969).

subjects brought before the Council have been treated too superficially and too seldom in the ordinary run of preaching. Nevertheless it can hardly be denied that what can be culled in the way
of opinion contributed from below has indeed been gained—a
not inconsiderable merit, when it comes to the question of introducing a more democratic model of administration into what
from a sociological viewpoint is by tradition a strictly closed hierarchical system.

Translated by Hubert Hoskins

PART II
DOCUMENTATION
CONCILIUM

Bärbel Kopetzky and Robert Baer

Students and the Democratization of the Church

TODAY democracy and democratization have become catchwords which mean everything or nothing. Constant and increasing use of these terms seems to lead to a diminution of their content and value. Democratization was the original slogan of the student revolts of 1968 and 1969. But this demand was very quickly taken up by other social groups. Talk of democratization is heard more and more in the Churches as well. In this issue of *Concilium* an attempt has been made to get to grips with this demand, to inquire into its theological justification, and to see how—with certain emphases and qualifications—it can be appplied to the Church.

Various parties have repeatedly asserted that Catholic student communities could serve as the model for a democratic Church structure.[1] Democratic experiments ought to be carried out in these sectors, because these are groups that are still least adapted to the existing form of society. Although it is not stated expressly, there is every reason to assume that these communities are thought of as an *élite* society and as the *avant-garde* of the Church. In this documentation we shall try to describe salient features of the student communities and to answer the question of whether they actually justify the hopes placed in them. By reference to the relevant literature and personal experience, we shall attempt to give a picture of what is happening in the student communities

[1] Cf. *"Neue Kirchen strukturen? Umfrage unter Studentengemeinden"*, *Diakonia*, 4 (1969), pp. 193 ff.; N. Greinacher, *"Hochschulgemeinde als Experiment"*, *Diakonia*, 4 (1969), pp. 321 ff.

in Western Europe, and to indicate the factors determining their present course of development. We have also included a short report by a student chaplain from the United States. Unfortunately, practical considerations have prevented the inclusion of additional reports from other continents. Even though we are conscious of the restricted frame of reference of this documentation, and that developments in universities throughout the world proceed at such a pace that any judgments must be soon outdated in part, the similarities between tendencies in different areas do, we think, allow it wider relevance.[2]

I. WHAT IS A STUDENT COMMUNITY?

Catholic church law does not provide for anything of the kind, and most reference books are of little or no help in this respect. Even the German *Handbuch der Pastoraltheologie* contains—and in the 1968 edition—no more than an article on the pastoral care of students.[3]

Student chaplaincies in this regard date back to the nineteenth century. But in the difficult economic conditions of the inter-war period a so-called *Studenten-Sorge* developed in Germany, which was concerned not so much with the spiritual aspect of student life in terms of individual souls, as with students' practical needs. The National-Socialist dictatorship abolished all confessional organizations among students, and allowed Catholic and Evangelical student chaplains to carry on only a sacramental ministry and to expound Scripture. Small circles evolved around these chaplains and after the war became centres of a new community life. Universities recognized these as Evangelical and Catholic "student communities", or "parishes", as did the respective Churches, which also entrusted them with the pastoral care of students.

These communities or chaplaincies came to see the centre of their concern in the universities and institutes themselves, and not so much in providing a point of spiritual recourse for

[2] Cf. the special issue of *Esprit*, 37 (May 1969), *La révolte des étudiants dans le monde*.

[3] W. Ruf, *"Studentenseelsorge"*, in *Handbuch der Pastoraltheologie*, III (Freiburg, 1968), pp. 268–301.

students *from* the university. They had a duty as well in taking up a position and showing commitment in questions of university politics. In addition, people from other levels of university life began to join the communities, so that they became representative not only of the students but of all sectors. After this short introduction, we shall try to describe the position of the university communities in greater detail; however, the reader must remember that despite the general interest in them manifested by the mass media in Germany, very few well-documented accounts have as yet appeared.

II. Evangelical Student Communities in Germany

The book on "Students and the Church" edited by H. Ringeling and H. C. Rohrbach contains eleven essays and a documentary appendix showing how Evangelical chaplaincies have developed in the last twenty-five years.[4] Most of the authors have tried to bring out the quite individual trend during this period, yet by and large they show a student community that is only a few steps ahead of the Church as a whole. Among features of special significance there are supra-confessionalism with respect to the different Evangelical Churches in Germany,[5] liturgical experimentation,[6] ecumenical contacts with the Catholic Church,[7] abolition of the clerical structure of community management,[8] and political recognition of the existence of two German States.[9] These developments have been for the most part fortuitous, and until the end of the nineteen-fifties the Evangelical communities saw their

[4] *Studenten und die Kirche* (Wuppertal, 1968), cf. Editor's instruction. See also the detailed review by R. Tietz, *"Zur Situation der Studentengemeinden"*, in *Wissenschaft und Praxis in Kirche u. Ges.*, 59 (1970), pp. 245-54.
[5] See C. Bartels, *"Konfession: Studentengemeinde"*, in *Studenten und die Kirche*, pp. 13-24.
[6] See J. Braun, *"Studentischer Gottesdienst als Lebenszentrum der Gemeinde"*, in *op. cit.*, pp. 25-31.
[7] See K. Engelhardt, *"Evangelisch-katholische Ökumene in den Studentengemeinden"*, in *op. cit.*, pp. 117-35.
[8] K. Birkhölzer, *"Die Struktur der Gemeindeleitung"*, in *op. cit.*, pp. 117-35.
[9] See M. Schröter, *"Evangelische Studentengemeinde—in welchem Deutschland?"* in *op. cit.*, pp. 148-69.

main task as the organization of leisure activities, since opportunities in this area of university life were very restricted.

The decisive point of renewal came with the recognition of the
communities' real place in the universities, and in particular in
the process of confrontation with the problem of specialist studies.
The gradual displacement of the concept of "general studies" in
favour of individual specialisms produced a situation in which
scholarship or science could no longer be conceived as "pure"
but only as "applied sciences"—knowledge and science as technology. The problem of the freedom of knowledge came to the
fore, and it became clear that the results of research were being
used by a small minority as instruments of social domination.
The Evangelical student communities saw (and see) themselves
as faced with the problem of science in society as one which con-
fronts all their members theoretically and—later on, in the pur-
suit of their professions—in practice. It is in this context that they
have to interpret and live Christian concepts like freedom, conciliation and true knowledge. They try to resolve this problem
structurally by pursuing their task in study and work groups in
which freshmen and mature students are separated, and pro-
fessors and lecturers are co-workers. The charismatic chaplains
who were once the sole leaders of the student groups give way to
the new student community, crystallizing out of the process of
dialogue between different groups, and seeing itself as an "exodus
community"—i.e., one living the life of hope in a redeemed
society of the future.

III. The Political Community—The Berlin Ecumenical Group

In order to particularize, we shall relate the history of some individual groups in short. In the Free University of Berlin (West),
the Catholic and Evangelical student community developed from
a conformist model to the point of solidarity with the left-wing
university groups, and thence to the condition of a "political
community"—as their former chaplain K.-B. Hasselmann puts
it.[10] Today this community includes Catholic and Evangelical

[10] See the documentation *Politische Gemeinde* (*Konkretionen*, Vol. 7)
(Hamburg, 1969).

students, since the Roman Catholic Bishop of Berlin no longer recognizes the Catholic student organization as such.[11] After the many demonstrations and protests in the University in 1968/69 it is now relatively quiet in Berlin. The community has dissociated itself from the revolutionary ideas of the APO and is looking for its own ways of reaching the common goal. It would like to provide a neutral platform for discussions of the various directions and in this way realize something like reconciliation. In any case, there is a disinclination to fix ideological principles and tendencies in advance.[12] In place of a general social commitment, the community tends towards dialogue with the individual sciences and subjects of study by means of which the future problems of our society are critically analysed. This reorientation also produced an alteration of structure: the attainment of community, inasmuch as the student chaplain was replaced by a team representing various faculties and subjects. The next few years will surely show that this idea was the right one, even though there is the danger of a kind of "starvation into submission" from the Right and the Left.

IV. An Unsuccessful Experiment in Bochum

At the new Ruhr University of Bochum, during the winter term of 1967/68, together with the student chaplain eight students took over the management of the Catholic student community.[13] The students had prepared for their task by analysing the nature of last-stage capitalism and studying the Marxist critique of religion. They wanted to reveal reactionary Catholicism as a political factor in the Federal Republic, for they were convinced that this aspect had received too little attention in the student movement.

---

[11] M. Krämer, *"Die KHG-Westberlin"*, in *Kritischer Katholizismus*, 3 (1970), Nos. 7/8, pp. 7 ff.
[12] K.-B. Hasselmann, *op. cit.*, pp. 159–60.
[13] On the following points, see the reports of the members of the Bochum student community: Hermann Böckenförde and M. Stankowski, *"Vom Ritual zur Information—Studentengemeinde als 'trojanisches Pferd'"*, in *Kritischer Katholizismus* (Frankfurt, 1969), pp. 74–82, esp. pp. 79 ff., and H. Hücking and F. v.f. Oudenrjn, *"KSG Bochum, model van een bevrijding van de kerk van zichzelf"*, *Tegenspraak*, 1 (1970, No. 4), pp. 49–54.

They looked on their work not only as a critique of the Church but as a critique of society. Consequently they very soon came into contact with left-wing political student groups and methods of co-operation. They experimented with new forms of divine service in the sense of a socially directed proclamation of the Gospel. They also tried to get in touch with the local parishes, clergy and religion teachers—but in general failed in this respect, just as the revolutionary students had failed in their attempts to co-operate with the workers. This new programme very soon found many sympathizers, but on the other hand encountered resistance from students (of theology) who took only a religious and sacramental interest in the student parish. An emotional polarization occurred which made dialogue impossible. At the end of the winter term the team had to retire; through the efforts of the chaplain concerned and the Essen church administration a slow change in the position of the community was begun. The new goal of the community is, according to Father Ehm: "I don't want a right- or left-wing, but a Christian community."[14] The members of the team offer a positive assessment of their experiences. They believe that this development of the student community contributed to opening the way to their emancipation from the Church and religion.[15]

At the time of writing, the construction of a church centre in Bochum is being planned, in which the Catholic and Evangelical parish and student community will be brought together under one roof.[16] It is hoped that this will—with the students' help—advance the process of enlightenment in local parishes. It remains to be seen whether the students will succeed in making the local parish dynamic, or—on the contrary—the student community will be paralysed.

V. The Amsterdam Student "Ecclesia"

We shall follow up these two German examples with one from Holland—the (Catholic) student *"ecclesia"* of Amsterdam. First of all, it must be remarked that the Amsterdam situation is not

---

[14] *Krit. Kath.*, 2 (1969), No. 3, p. 4.
[15] Böckenförde-Stankowski, *loc. cit.*, p. 82.
[16] M. Bourrée, *"Kirche unter einem Dach"*, *Publik*, 11 (Sept. 1970), p. 32.

typical of the other Dutch student communities. Certain definite tendencies have appeared there which are not apparent in any other university. Nevertheless, this particular case reveals current dangers which threaten them all.

The Amsterdam community won some notoriety on account of its liturgical experiments, its critical standpoint with regard to dogmas of the Catholic Church, and finally its protest against compulsory clerical celibacy.[17] It conceived itself as on the edge of the official Church. On the one hand, it did not want to break with the institutional Church, but wished to acknowledge its norms as little as possible. The community is highly respected for its qualitatively superlative energy, which is taken as a model by many ordinary parishes. Since 28 September 1970, when a married priest said Mass publicly in the students' chapel, the Bishop of Haarlem has disclaimed responsibility for the group. His rejection of the community was followed by an announcement that the chapel was withdrawn from their use, and finally by cessation of financial support by the *Radboudstiftung*.

The reaction to these events has been relatively weak. The other student chaplains have regretted that this step was taken unilaterally and without reference to other communities. One might well ask whether this is not the termination of a development long under way—namely, the isolation of the community both from the official Church and from the University. An investigation on 2 February 1969, for instance, showed that the majority of those attending student services did not come from university circles.[18] This trend has most probably grown in the meantime. It must be remarked that the *"ecclesia"* did not take part in the student troubles of 1969, but clearly abstained from engagement in university politics. An analysis of its mode of proclamation[19] shows it to be romantic and contemplative. Sermons were addressed to the individual, describing and playing on his difficulties and conflicts, but avoiding any attempt to analyse them. Consolation is afforded the individual as an

[17] For the Amsterdam events, see L. Roy *et al.*, *Ein Modell von Kirche?* (Düsseldorf, 1969).
[18] Quoted according to W. Jansen and J. Nagel, *"Een oase in de hoofdstad"*, *Tegenspraak*, 1 (1970), No. 4, p. 38.
[19] *Ibid.*, pp. 39–40.

individual. He is to win his freedom from the powers by acquitting himself alone. The functions of the community are largely restricted to liturgical celebration and assistance in individual cases.[20]

VI. Structural Reform of the French "Mission Etudiante" and "Action Catholique Universitaire"

In France, the pastoral care of students is entrusted to "centres" attached to the individual Faculties. These centres are largely concerned with liturgical celebrations, and also engage in missionary activity among students.[21] In addition, there is the Christian student union (J.E.C.), whose university section became self-sufficient in 1966 as the *"Action catholique universitaire"*.[22] This movement wished to become an active element in the student environment and to proceed from the given concerns and situation of the students themselves. Even before the famous May events of 1968 the *"Mission Etudiante"* was concerned to produce an analysis of "reality as lived by students of the present".[23]

This report offers confirmation that "the community far too often presents the image of the comfortable believer". The great majority of those who have questions to ask no longer expect any answer from their parishes. The conclusion is drawn for the parishes and communities of the Church that they should not draw up any kind of Christian system which is above men's heads, but must proceed from the basis of the life actually lived by men.

This development was overtaken by the May events, in which the Catholic students also took part. They joined the various groups concerned, or departed for movements outside the universities. Various students tried to bring the revolution into the

[20] That the Amsterdam student church is an extreme case is shown by the analysis of other Dutch communities (Tilburg, Groningen and Heerlen) and of the Belgian community at Louvain in *Tegenspraak, loc. cit.* They are much more strongly related to the actual university and social situation of Holland and Belgium.

[21] W. Ruf, *"Studentenseelsorge"*, in *Lex f. Theol. u. Kirche*, IX (Freiburg, 1964), p. 1118.

[22] Cf. on the following, P. Moulinier, *"L'église dans l'université française aujourd'hui"*, in *Inform. cath. intern*, No. 353 (Feb. 1970), pp. 23-31.

[23] *Ibid.*, p. 27.

Church, but this was for the most part not held to be a task of primary importance, and treated as a sign of clericalism.

During the May events, students discovered the political dimension of their activity and of their common interests in university politics. They asked themselves what function the particular Christian communities could perform in those events. Did they not support an a-political mode—the maintenance of the existing political order through the very activities they took part in: Masses, pilgrimages, and so on? Many small groups discussed the consequences for the Church among students.

After the introduction of the university reforms, the student unions experienced a substantial loss, which was also felt in the student mission. At present the "informal groups" are the liveliest in France; among them are groups which are highly committed politically, prayer groups, and groups interested in theology and Bible study. During 1970 one could discern a slight movement towards structural reform, as a new generation entered the universities. The next two years will show what direction is eventually taken. At present they are thinking things through.[24]

VII. STUDENT CHAPLAINCY IN THE UNITED STATES

Until recent years the educational ideal of American Catholicism appeared unreal and defensive, namely, "every Catholic in a Catholic school". This attitude could be detected in the amazing multiplication of Catholic school facilities on the one hand, and the pastoral neglect of Catholics who for various reasons attended secular schools, on the other hand. Nowhere was this latter truth more apparent than on the university level.

In the academic year 1963–64, for example, there were 2,100 colleges and universities in America of which 295 were Catholic. The ratio of full-time priest to Catholic student on the secular campuses was about one priest to 3,100 Catholics, while Catholic campuses had a ratio of one priest or religious to 35 students. According to the survey of Clifford and Callahan, 2 out of 3

[24] *Ibid.*, p. 31. In this connection, one should also consider the question of a renewed school and youth chaplaincy, cf. A. Savard, *"Dans les lycées français: une nouvelle aumonerie,* in *Inf. cath. int.,* No. 360 (May 1970), pp. 24–31, and L. de Vaucelles, "Les mutations de la J.E.C.", in *Etudes* (Aug./Sept. 1970), pp. 278–86.

Catholic students were at that time enrolled in the secular universities.[25]

In contrast to the Catholic university, which represented a great investment of religious personnel and church finances, as well as having the moral support of the church leadership, the Catholic students at the state university or college were viewed with grave misgivings. "They should not be there in the first place", was a frequent criticism from pastors who should have known better. The minister appointed to serve their needs was often a part-time chaplain whose main responsibility was in connection with a neighbouring parish. Lacking any previous training or adequate educational background, the chaplain not infrequently tended to treat the Catholic university community as another parish society.

Fortunately many chaplains transcended their initial shortcomings, and responded admirably to the challenges of this unusual apostolate.

Early in the 1960s, the great universities began to be recognized as the truly creative centres in American society. Their creativity was seen more in terms of technology, however. They were the great forces speeding technological development, and consequently the Government and private enterprise both poured vast sums of research money into the universities. Catholic institutions of learning benefited very modestly from the windfall because they were not equipped for rapid expansion, and because of the time-honoured separation of Church and State in America. This drew still greater numbers of Catholic students to secular campuses.

Some church leaders began to read the prognoses and to pay serious attention to the needs of the Catholic students on the secular campuses. Cardinal Cushing of Boston was a good example of a church leader who moved from a defensive posture to a very positive and progressive one regarding the secular universities, which formed such an important part of his archdiocese. In a sermon at the dedication of the Catholic Centre at Massachusetts State University in 1963, he acknowledged that "a most critical area for the apostolate of the Church in the United States is the world of the secular university campus".

[25] R. J. Clifford and W. R. Callahan, "Catholics in Higher Education", in *America* (Sept. 1964).

Emphasizing the positive goal of Catholic education, he said: "The work of the University Apostolate must go beyond an attempt to save the faith. It must do more than produce well-informed Catholics. . . . Rather it must make well-formed Catholics." The elements of this total formation he described as worship, education, experience of community and responsible action following upon this experience. These ideas were a further refining of the traditional spiritual, educational and social goals of the Newman Apostolate, the name given to the secular campus ministry among Catholics in the past.

The Catholic chaplain on the secular campus in many ways anticipated the new directions of Vatican II. The religiously pluralistic world of the State University prodded him immediately into deep ecumenical dialogue and co-operative action with other campus ministers. In contrast, the Catholic campus seemed like a carefully controlled ghetto. A meaningful liturgy was of pressing importance for the minister on the secular campus, because his students would not respond otherwise. Consequently he was experimenting with liturgical innovations in advance of Vatican II, and some of the most expressive and satisfying liturgies today are found in the Catholic community on the secular campus. The tensions between ecumenism and convert work, between free intellectual inquiry and censorship, between mixed religious marriages and Catholic marriages required practical resolution on the part of the campus minister long before Vatican II gave him direction or moral support.

In the middle 1960s students in the State Universities sparked off a dramatic change in the relationship of university to society. One might superficially describe the change by saying that the universities moved from being centres of creation to centres of disruption. What was happening was really an awakening on the part of university students to their responsibility in the process of social change not only in the university world, but in society at large. A landmark in this development was the Free Speech Movement at the University of California at Berkeley. It was followed by student involvement with social causes such as racial injustice, the Vietnam War, conscientious objection to military conscription, and the relation of Federal Government and university, to mention only a few.

Once again the campus minister was on the front line of change. For several years now he has been increasingly called upon to give moral witness and leadership in social progress, in addition to all the traditional forms of pastoral care. He must now spend a good portion of his time counselling those facing the military draft, and trying to heal the increasing polarization of alienation which is taking place in the university as well as in society in general. One chaplain reported recently that because of the steady stream of bomb threats at his campus, averaging 15 per day, he has been devoting much attention to counselling the students on how best to live and study in the midst of such continual harassment

The secular campus chaplains have had to become a resourceful group of ministers, extremely sensitive to the spiritual needs of their students and acutely perceptive of the fast and profound changes in the university and society that have swept through America. Until recently the training for such an important assignment has been very weak or non-existent for the few hundred full-time chaplains. A hopeful sign for the future is the newly reported plan for a National Center for Campus Ministry to be opened in Boston in 1971. According to its co-directors, Father Robert Bullock and Laurence Murphy, three basic things will take place at the center. There will be the preparation of campus ministers with new kinds of educational techniques, including a good supervisory internship programme. There will be a continuing education programme in which people from all over the country will be invited to lecture for brief periods on some particular issues, and there will be research and planning. The centre will be open to men and women of various Christian denominations who are involved in or intend to join a ministry in higher education on Catholic or secular campuses.

VIII. Democracy and the Student Community

After this attempt to describe the situation of individual communities and student pastoral work, we return to the theme of the democratization of the Church. In his introductory article, H. Schneider has asserted that at present various conceptions of democracy exist alongside one another (Western and Eastern

models, the types favoured in the developing countries). Formally, democratization means an increase of self-determination
and a decrease of alien determination, which can be realized and
institutionalized in a multiplicity of forms.

In many university communities, students have for a long
time tried to achieve new democratic structures. In West Germany, for example, each community has long enjoyed its own
particular, more or less democratic, statutes. Nevertheless, the
student chaplains have for a long time alone controlled the way
taken by their communities, for they were often the only ones
who could ensure continuity. In addition, the choice of students
holding office was often purely fortuitous; they could never enjoy
the support of the whole community, which was not active as
such. In a formal perspective these communities were to some
extent democratic, yet very far removed from the process of
democratization. Translated into terms of communication theory,
democratization means: "unimpeded, multilateral and free dialogue", and, negatively, "the purely monological type of living
and decision-making", with borderline-cases on either side.[26]

Applied to the student communities, this means that during
the student troubles they entered into a new phase—that of dialogue, of communication with the other sectors of the University
—by taking part in the protests, demonstrations, and so on. In
this process, they realized that a Christian community cannot
proclaim the Christian Gospel abstractly, without any reflection
of its function in the University and of the relation of the University to society; and cannot conceive of itself as the holy remnant
in a now pagan world. It will be its task to help forward the
realization in the University and in society of fraternity, freedom
and reconciliation by producing them out of hope in a reconciled
society. If a Christian community wants to achieve this end, it
can do it only through dialogue and engagement in the University. It can no longer stand apart. From this, structural conclusions are to be drawn as well: the community can no longer
distinguish itself clearly from the University and other student
groups.[27]

[26] H. Schneider, "Democracy: The Idea and the Reality", at the end of
his article in this issue.
[27] See K. Birkhölzer, *loc. cit.*, pp. 120 ff.

For example, the reorientation of the West Berlin student community enabled it to replace a single chaplain with a team of specialists from various sectors of the University.[28] It is hoped that they will lead to a broadening of the vanguard of the community and a concretization of its work in regard to the individual specialisms of the University, in order thus to advance mutual dialogue and to stimulate communication between students and other university elements with reference to science and society, in order ultimately to arrive at conscious actions capable of actually bringing about change.

IX. Conclusions

We should now like to raise the question of the significance of this development towards a conscious university community in regard to a democratization of the Church. In the first place, there is an obvious sort of trigger action to be expected from the student communities. Just as the stimulus for the present surge of democratization in all areas of society came from students, so the same effect occurred in the Church. In this respect there was the intervention of the *"Kritischer Katholikentag"* at the Essen *Katholikentag* in 1968, which was planned by various student groups.[29]

In view of the recent events at universities in Western Europe, it is nevertheless no longer so probable that students will provoke stimuli and interventions towards democratization to the same extent as in the past. After the official reforms in the universities, the situation there has become perceptibly quieter, and anyway people have tired of the many demonstrations. Other social groups (trade unions, political parties, etc.) will take the place of students, and—correspondingly—clerical and lay organizations will become more active in the Church.

In addition to the key-stimulus function, the student communities will be able to attain to the significance of a model for the Church, to the extent that the local parish communities, following the example of the university communities, discover their place and function in a particular town, village or county. They

[28] K.-B. Hasselmann, *op. cit.*
[29] Cf. *Herderkorrespondenz* 22 (1968), pp. 469–72.

will no longer be able to withdraw from the problems of environmental pollution, the inhospitality of our cities, the impoverishment of entire sections of the population and of social intercourse, which threaten the future of mankind. They will be required to engage in communication, in dialogue with other groups, in order to analyse existing conditions and to change them through action. It will be necessary to translate the Christian Gospel into the actual situation, to submit one's own Church's practice to its critical measure, and actively to contribute to the liberation of mankind on the spot. A sign of movement in this direction is the positive assessment of the unrest among Catholics.[30] It is quite possible that this process of slow coming to consciousness will be accelerated by the forthcoming national Synods in the United States and the Federal Republic; on the other hand, we must hope that the student communities and parishes do not follow the example of the Amsterdam student *"ecclesia"* and regress to a peculiar subjectivity.

[30] See the response to the questionnaire on the Synod in the Federal Republic. Only 18·2% regret the development: *Publik* (Dec. 1970), p. 21.

Translated by John Griffiths

Biographical Notes

NORBERT GREINACHER was born 26 April 1931 at Freiburg-im-Breisgau and ordained in 1956. He studied at the Universities of Freiburg, Paris and Vienna. Doctor of theology, he is professor of pastoral theology at the University of Tübingen. Among his published works are: *Die Kirche in der stadtischen Gesellschaft* (Mainz, 1966) and, in collaboration, *Bilanz des deutschen Katholizismus* (Mainz, 1966).

PETER HUIZING, S.J., was born 22 February 1911 at Haarlem and ordained in 1942. He studied at the Universities of Amsterdam, Nijmegen, Louvain and Munich and at the Gregorian, Rome. Licentiate in philosophy and in theology, doctor of civil law and of canon law, he is professor of canon law and of the history of canon law at the University of Nijmegen, and also consultor to the Roman Commission for the Revision of the Code of Canon Law. Among his published works is *De Trentse huwelijksvorm* (Hilversum/Antwerp, 1966).

JAN KERKHOFS, S.J., was born 15 May 1924 at Basselt (Belgium) and ordained in 1956. He studied at the Jesuit Faculty of Theology at Louvain and at the Universities of Louvain and Oxford. Licentiate in philosophy and in theology and doctor of sociology, he is secretary general of Pro Mundi Vita and professor of pastoral sociology at the Higher Institute of Religious Sciences at Louvain University. His published works include: *Godsdienstpraktijk en social milieu* (Brussels, 1954) and, in collaboration, *De Kerk in Vlaandersen* (Tielt, 1962).

RAYMUND KOTTJE was born 23 December 1926 at Düsseldorf and was ordained in 1954. He studied at the Universities of Cologne, Munich and Bonn. Doctor of theology, he is professor of Church history at the University of Regensburg. Among his published works is *Einfluss des Alten Testamentes auf Recht und Liturgie des frühen Mittelalters* (Bonn, 1970²).

KARL LEHMANN was born 16 May 1936 at Sigmaringen and was ordained in 1963. He studied at the Universities of Freiburg-im-Breisgau and Munich and at the Gregorian, Rome. Licentiate in theology, doctor of philosophy and of theology, he is professor of dogmatics at the University of Mainz. Among his published works is *Auferweckt am dritten Tag nach der Schrift* (Freiburg-im-B., 1968).

RUDOLF PESCH was born 2 September 1936 at Bonn. He studied at the Universities of Bonn and Freiburg-im-Breisgau. Doctor of philosophy (1964), doctor of theology (1967), he is scientific assistant at the Seminary of Exegesis of the Department of the New Testament at the University of Freiburg. Among his published works are: *Die kirchlich-politische Presse der Katholiken der Rheinprovinz vor 1848* (Mainz, 1966) and *Die Vision des Stephanus* (SBS 12) (Stuttgart, 1966).

JEAN REMY was born at Soumagne (Belgium) in 1928. He studied at Louvain University. Licentiate in philosophy and doctor of economic sciences, he is assistant lecturer at the Faculty of Political and Social Sciences at Louvain University and director of the *section francophone* of the Centre of Socio-Religious Research at the same university. Among his published works are: "Famille et relations personnelles en milieu urbain" in *Le Phénomène humain* (Paris, 1965) and *Milieu urbain et communauté chrétienne* (Paris, 1968).

HEINRICH SCHNEIDER was born 10 August 1929 at Brandenburg/Havel (Austria) and is a Catholic. He studied philosophy and theology at the School of Higher Education at Bamberg and then went on to Munich University and the Western Reserve University at Cleveland. Doctor of philosophy, he is professor of political philosophy and critique of ideology at Vienna University. He has written several articles on political theory, European integration, etc.